GW00570510

SUZUKI GSX-R A LEGACY OF PERFORMANCE

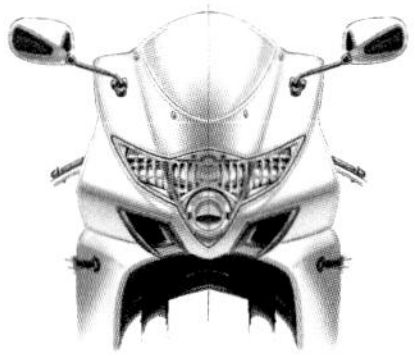

SUZUKI
GSX
SUZUKI
TOKICO

A LEGACY OF PERFORMANCE

BY MARC COOK FOREWORD BY KEVIN SCHWANTZ

DESIGN BY TOM MORGAN

Library of Congress Control Number: 2005922096

ISBN: 1 893618 51 X

Book and cover design: Blue Design (www.bluedes.com)
Portland, Maine

Printed in Hong Kong

10 9 8 7 6 5 4 3 2 1

David Bull Publishing
4250 East Camelback Road
Suite K150
Phoenix, AZ 85018

602-852-9500
602-852-9503 (fax)

www.bullpublishing.com

Photo Credits
The publisher would like to thank all the artists who contributed to this book. While a large part of the photography was provided by Suzuki Motor Corporation in Japan and American Suzuki Motor Corporation, and the author, the following photographers also contributed their work:
Shigeo Kibiki: Page 11-14, 19, 24, 26, 31, 32, 40-41, 43, 47, 54, 64, 68, 90-91, 94-95, 114-115, 137-139, 151 (top, above left)
Brian J Nelson: Page 10, 138 (right), 139 (left), 149, 150 (above), 151 (above left, below left, above right)
Kevin Wing: Page 92, 163, 191
Tom Riles: Page 112

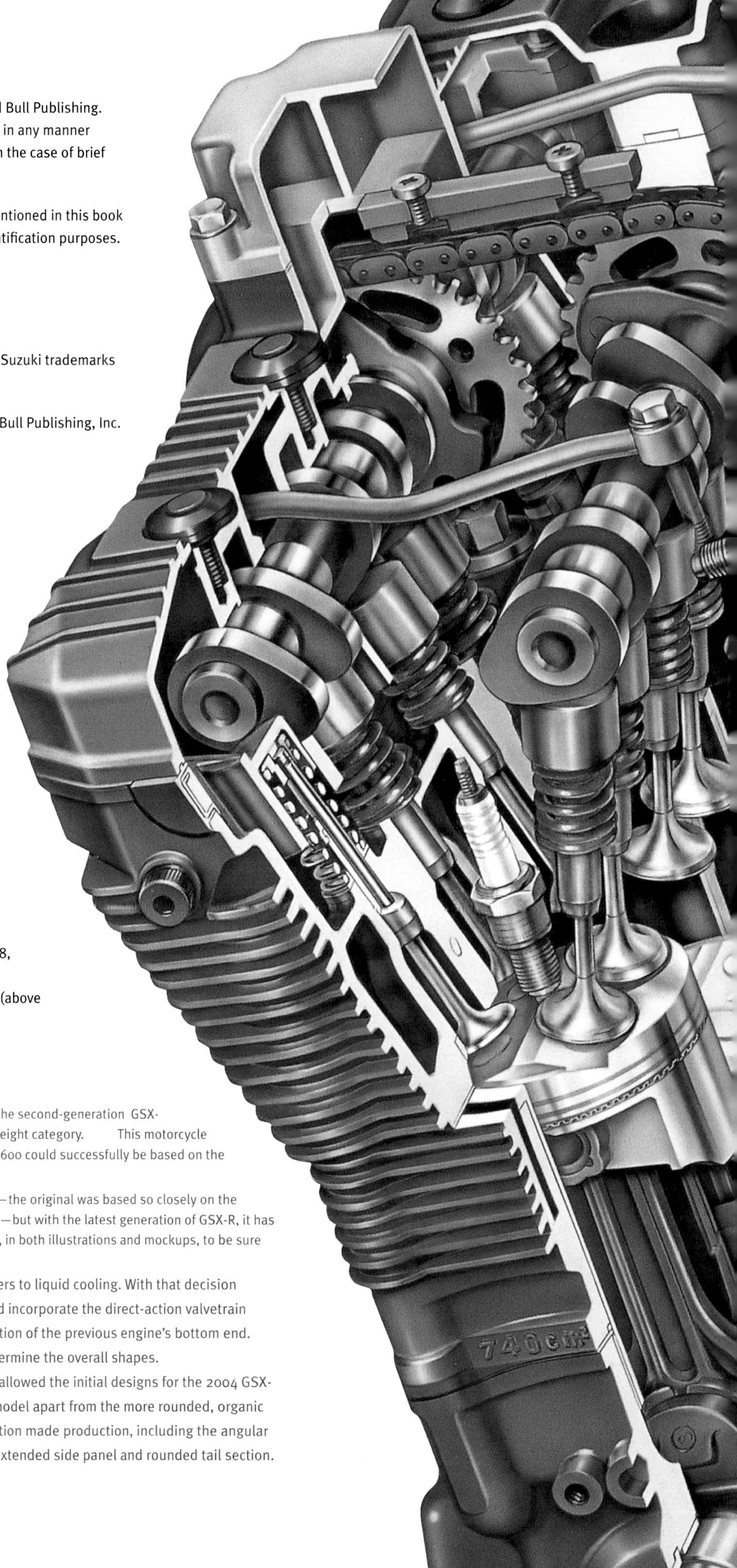

PAGE 2: Resplendent in traditional blue-and-white Suzuki racing livery, the second-generation GSX-R600 represents the company's best foray into the hard-fought middleweight category. This motorcycle also showed the great advantages of modular engineering, in which the 600 could successfully be based on the 750.

PAGE 3: Styling has always been an important part of the GSX-R design—the original was based so closely on the endurance-race-winning GS1000R that it could almost be mistaken for it—but with the latest generation of GSX-R, it has become nearly an obsession. Numerous styling designs have been tried, in both illustrations and mockups, to be sure the latest version is both handsome and true to the GSX-R's heritage.

PAGE 4: It was the push for more horsepower that drove the engineers to liquid cooling. With that decision made, they could reduce the size of the cylinder block and head and incorporate the direct-action valvetrain they had wanted to use two years before—and still retain a fair portion of the previous engine's bottom end.

PAGE 6: The GSX-R is tested in the tunnel with a rider aboard to determine the overall shapes.

PAGE 8: New ideas, new directions but a continuing clarity of focus allowed the initial designs for the 2004 GSX-R600 and GSX-R750 to reach for a fresh, angular look that set the model apart from the more rounded, organic styling of the previous generation. Many of the ideas in this illustration made production, including the angular headlight and ram-air treatment, while others did not, namely the extended side panel and rounded tail section.

Table of Contents

GSX-R
Team
SUZUKI
Kevin Schwantz
SUZUKI
genuine accessories
SUZUKI

FOREWORD

By Kevin Schwantz

Has it been twenty years already? I'm delighted to help the GSX-R celebrate this important anniversary because both the bike and Suzuki itself have been so much a part of my racing career. And now, of course, my school uses Suzuki sportbikes exclusively, so I've had the opportunity to watch the development of the GSX-R from its earliest days as the ground-breaking race-replica sportbike to the incredible machine it continues to be today.

There is no doubt in my mind that the Suzuki GSX-R was well ahead of its time. I remember hearing a lot about the bike and then seeing photos in early 1985, thinking, "Wow, this is an amazing-looking street bike." I could tell that it would translate well into a race bike, but I also thought that it would be a big change from the bike I had been riding for Yoshimura in 1985, the GS700E. Because the GSX-R was not brought to America in 1985, I was still riding the Yoshimura GS.

I believe we tend to look back on that period of AMA Superbike racing and think that the bikes were less developed than they are now, even a bit crude. At the time, I didn't think so. When I came into the Yoshimura team, it all seemed incredibly exciting and I was just happy to be there, working for a well-run team that had good equipment. My goals and strategy were pretty simple: take it day by day and win races.

I always got along with the GS700E. I'd come from motocross and dirt track, and so I liked the big handlebar. The bike, to me, was an absolute hoot to ride. It would do what I wanted it to do, went where I wanted it to go. I wouldn't say finesse was a big part of my style then, but my style seemed to work well on the GS. We won the second race of 1985 at Willow Springs and picked up two more wins later in the year. I think the fact that Yoshimura had a year of development on the 750cc bike before I got there really helped.

In 1985, I got to ride the GSX-R750 for the first time in a 200-kilometer race with Graeme Crosby as preparation for the Suzuka 8 Hours. I was immediately impressed with the bike's performance, even if it was a big change for me going to clip-on handlebars from big, dirt bike-style handlebars.

OPPOSITE: After Kevin Schwantz had proven himself in AMA Superbike racing, he moved full-time to the 500 Grand Prix class with Suzuki in 1988. By his retirement in 1995 he had earned 25 GP wins, 21 lap records, 29 pole positions, and won the 1993 World Championship. Such was his stature in the sport that the FIM, the sanctioning body, retired his number 34—the first time any rider had been honored this way. Schwantz continues to work with Suzuki as an advisor to the Yoshimura Suzuki team and through the Kevin Schwantz Suzuki School.

BELOW: A much younger—and exceptionally hungry—Schwantz raced his heart out for Yoshimura Suzuki starting in 1984. The 1986 racing season was Yoshimura's first with the GSX-R, but this "building year" paid off well for 1987, when Schwantz scored five wins aboard the Yoshimura-prepped GSX-R.

OPPOSITE: Schwantz is aboard the RGV500 GP bike at Laguna Seca in 1989. The effortless acceleration of the light, powerful two-stroke race bike suited his all-out style but, just as important, it gave Suzuki's engineers valuable experience with motorcycles tuned to the extremes of technology.

BELOW: Engineering staff members worked extensively on the 500GP program and allowed that hard-earned knowledge to inform later GSX-Rs, which would carefully and effectively replicate the race bike's dimensions and weight distribution to good effect.

I would like to think I had a hand in the development of the bike through the Yoshimura team, which has always been very tightly aligned with the factory. During our first two seasons with the GSX-R750 race bike, we made many small changes and requested more. I was always impressed with the factory's response.

In 1986 and 1987, I rode the bike and we worked really hard to develop it. I could see that Suzuki was paying attention to our efforts because the '88 GSX-R had a lot of changes that we had introduced in the Yoshimura team the two years before. The '88 bike was much nicer to ride from a handling standpoint. Of course, that year I rode the GSX-R at Daytona in 1988 and won. I have to say that the win at Daytona in the 200 was, for Suzuki, almost as good as winning the championship. We went out and proved what we could do against bigger teams, and the win felt great.

In 1988 I was in Grand Prix racing full-time on the Suzuki RGV500. That year we managed to pick up two wins and came home a strong eighth in the championship. At the time, Suzuki was starting to use our feedback on the GP bike to help develop the GSX-R. We were working hard on aerodynamics and suspension technology, which was coming along rapidly. I'm sure that what we learned in GP was put back into the GSX-R.

It has been interesting to watch the development of the GSX-R. I remember the introduction of the 2000 GSX-R750 at Misano. World Superbike had been there for the last race of the year, and we were there for the press launch the following February. It was cold, around 40 degrees. But in spite of the compromised traction from the low temperatures, I was less than ten seconds off the WSB pole on a totally stock motorcycle. At one of the events tied to the launch, I told the assembled journalists that I'd offer a bet: Let's take this bike to Daytona just as it is. I don't even need a whole day, probably just an hour or so to get it set up. But I guarantee that I could take this motorcycle on DOT tires and set a time that would beat my pole in 1988. Totally stock bike, blinkers and all. Nobody argued with me or took the bet.

The GSX-R had, by then, progressed amazingly far. It was, right off the showroom floor, a better race bike than my fully prepared, factory-supported GSX-R of a dozen years earlier.

The pace of the GSX-R's development is, if anything, accelerating.

I've spent a lot of time on the 2005 GSX-R1000 and can tell you that it is awesome. I came back to American Suzuki and said, point blank, that if we at

Suzuki have anybody we support who's riding one of these new GSX-R1000s and not winning, there's something wrong with the rider. That bike is by far the best production motorcycle I've ever ridden on a racetrack. I couldn't make it do anything wrong. I never adjusted the suspension on the bikes I rode; just right out of the box, they were amazing. Everything about the bike was so good. The changes from the '04 model have made a massive improvement. This new bike is so light and agile it gives me that 750 feeling again. It has so much traction and responds so well. The engine pulls so well right from idle and never has a big hit in the powerband. As the bike starts to spin the back tire, it doesn't feel like it's going to get away. Instead, it feels like there's so much grip that the tire will start spitting asphalt, really digging a trench. It's just amazing to experience.

Suzuki has learned so much from racing—Superbikes, 500 GP, and MotoGP—and the company has kept this up over the years. I really can see where Suzuki has worked out solutions in racing and quickly applied them to the production bikes. That responsiveness and commitment is something I just don't see from other manufacturers.

So, happy birthday to the GSX-R. It has been an incredible experience for me to be involved with the bike early on and now with my school. And it's been an honor to be associated with Suzuki, a company that, I think, understands how to go racing and how to put lessons learned from the track right back into the product.

SUZUKI
34

CHAPTER 1

BEFORE THERE WAS A GSX-R

OPPOSITE: Before the GSX-R, lionhearted Superbike racers like Wes Cooley battled on 1000cc, steel-frame monsters whose performance had a lot more to do with acceleration than nimble handling. It wasn't until the GSX-R that the race/development/production bike loop fully closed.

Suzuki's first GSX-R, a motorcycle whose twentieth birthday we're here to celebrate, took the accepted engineering wisdom of year-to-year incremental improvement and blew the premise to pieces. The GSX-R burst onto the scene and set sportbike enthusiasts and magazine writers alike into a tizzy because it was impossibly light, amazingly powerful, and so artfully conceived that the worst of the complaints about it amounted to a whisper in a windstorm. Just as important, the GSX-R portrayed a clarity of focus and a depth of commitment to a concept that few bikes in history had ever presented. One glimpse, an eyeblink's awareness of the bike across a showroom floor or coming the other way on the road, and you knew exactly, precisely what it was. And what it was meant to do.

No compromises, no dilution.

This was a difficult task for a company that had always been so logical in the development of its products, and one that had fastidiously worked to make each model as useful and broadly appealing as possible. Remember, this is the company that built the GT750 two-stroke, a gentleman's recliner of a motorcycle smack in the day of Kawasaki's hair-whitening two-stroke triples. This was Suzuki's way: prepare thoroughly engineered vehicles that were durable and practical. Mature riders of the day loved the brand.

The beginnings of Suzuki's transformation from a conservative producer to a market leader first came with the Hans Muth-designed Katana 1100. This bike was sharklike, unusual, unrestrained, and controversial, but still conventionally engineered. That's to say it was no lighter nor more powerful than the big (and quite successful) GS-series motorcycles that came before. Think of it as provocative wrapping on a Christmas gift of woolly socks.

Suzuki, like all major motorcycle manufacturers, had been racing. The company had begun racing in 1953, when the 60cc Diamond Free won its class in the Mt. Fuji Hillclimb. In the modern era came Barry Sheene's 500GP championships in 1976 and 1977 on a Suzuki RG500. One of his bikes is in the

BELOW: Considered the father of the GSX-R, Etsuo Yokouchi pushed his engineering team to explore every option to make the company's radical new sportbike exceptionally light and powerful. Mr. Yokouchi, shown here in 2005 at the Suzuki Museum at the company's Hamamatsu headquarters, is compelling in his role as a charismatic visionary for the process of engineering excellence.

Suzuki Museum at the company headquarters in Hamamatsu, and it's frightening to consider how fast he went on what today appears to be spindly, rudimentary machinery. But it was fast and capable in its time.

Suzuki could seemingly do no wrong. In the U.S., with the help of Yoshimura Racing, Wes Cooley brought back-to-back AMA Superbike titles in 1979 and 1980 on a GS1000S Superbike. (Cooley was the first man to wrest the championship from the tireless Reg Pridmore, who had won it three times since the category's inception in 1976.) A pair of World Endurance titles followed in 1981 and 1982 on a bike called the GS1000R (or XR41) that would form the basis of the GSX-R.

The company's involvement in racing—as a factory team for 500GP and through the American arm of Yoshimura in AMA racing—provided valuable feedback to the engineers in Hamamatsu and, more important, gave them uncommonly powerful motivation and determination.

ABOVE: Radical designs have been part of GSX-R history from the start, and continue through the 2005 GSX-R1000, shown here in a dramatic styling illustration. A sense of dynamic motion must work on many levels: visually, in the context of aerodynamic efficiency and, of course, for packaging and performance.

RIGHT: Throughout the two decades of GSX-R development, Suzuki's styling designers worked tirelessly to create distinctive shapes on top of first-rate mechanicals. The avenues *not* taken illustrate a lot about how Suzuki viewed the model.

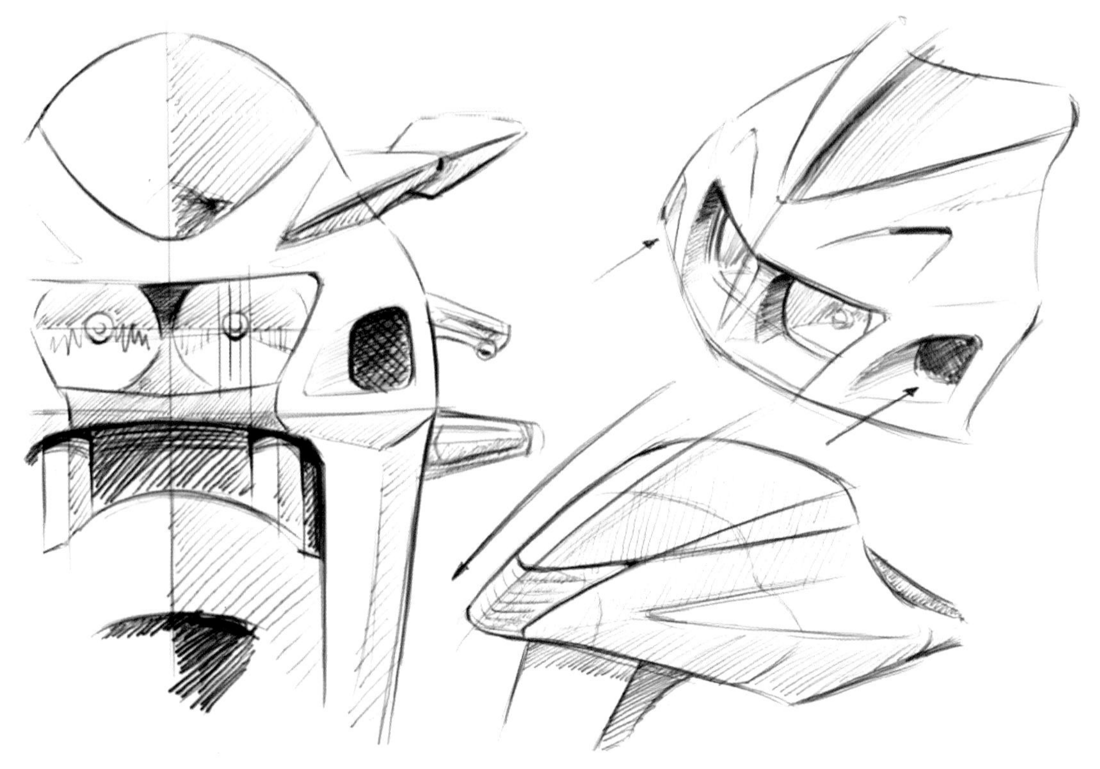

LEFT: Suzuki's first steps into the realm of superlight street bikes came in the form of the Japanese market 1983 RG250 Gamma, an aluminum-frame small-bore screamer that made enthusiastic Japanese riders grope for superlatives.

BELOW: In the mid-1990s, the GSX-R had a fully cemented reputation and clear market dominance in the 750 class. By the 1997 model, Suzuki was ready to once again challenge the 600 class; this RGV500-inspired model did so with aplomb.

ABOVE: Development of the GSX-R line has always taken place on the track as well as on the street. Whether it's at one of the famous venues in Europe or at the Ryuyo proving ground in Suzuki's own back yard, the development testing is relentless in searching for ultimate performance.

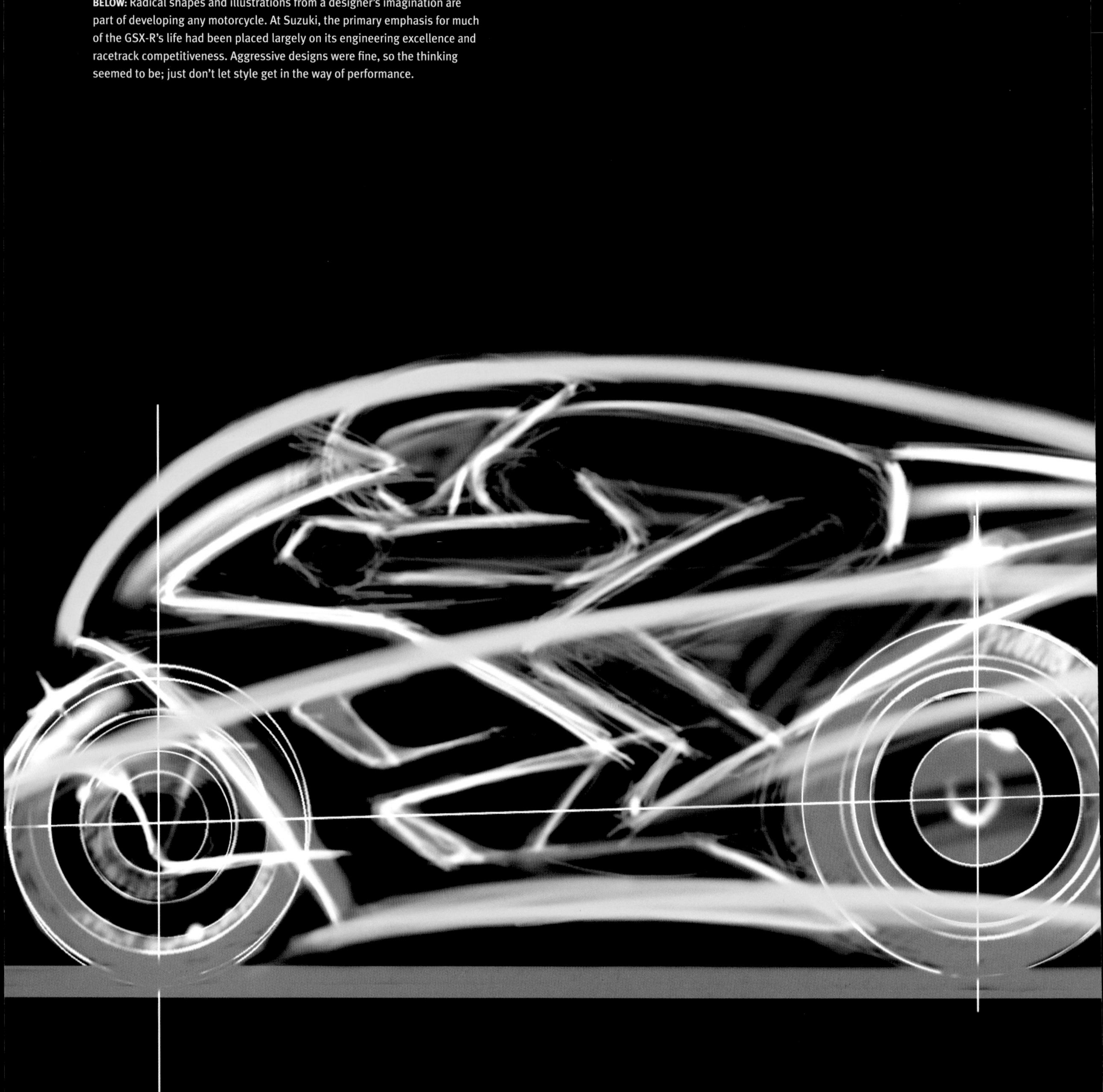

BELOW: Radical shapes and illustrations from a designer's imagination are part of developing any motorcycle. At Suzuki, the primary emphasis for much of the GSX-R's life had been placed largely on its engineering excellence and racetrack competitiveness. Aggressive designs were fine, so the thinking seemed to be; just don't let style get in the way of performance.

"Racing is a very important part of this company," says Sadayuki Inobe, the company's managing director. "It is part of our DNA."

With the introduction of the GSX-R, Suzuki's racing fortunes changed in ways unexpected. In AMA Superbike, the Yoshimura team won just a single championship (with Jamie James in 1989) until Mat Mladin set sail for his record five titles aboard the GSX-R750 and GSX-R1000. But something else happened. The GSX-R, "born on the circuit, returned to the circuit," according to then head of engineering Etsuo Yokouchi, would become the dominant bike for Superstock racing and for privateers all over the world. It was the closest thing to a race bike with lights and, as a result, the bike most easily turned into a competitive racer.

It is impossible to underestimate the effect of the GSX-R on Suzuki's fortunes. More than one executive has said that the company would not be what it is today without the success of the GSX-R. And success, in this case, is more than fiscal, although it can't be denied that the company's bottom line has done well by the sportbike.

No, the broader truth is that the GSX-R gave Suzuki a distinctive brand image and catapulted it from being a small manufacturer of fine and efficient but generally not world-champion motorcycles to its current guise as the sportbike powerhouse. The GSX-R drove Suzuki to the front of an emerging category precisely when the company most needed the boost.

Today, with an entirely new generation of engineers pushing the GSX-R line forward, the brand continues to shine. And although the relentless pace of technology has put the series on a shortened development cycle—one so short there's barely time enough to launch the product, take a breath, and look around to see how the competition is doing—working on the GSX-R is considered the highest honor inside the company. Every engineer, every styling designer, and every test rider who pounds around the Ryuyo test track in all weather views it as a plum assignment. Not easy work, but intensely worthwhile.

Each of the nearly forty men who were inter-

ABOVE: Design strategies ensured that the GSX-R's visual heritage was maintained while the bike was gently, carefully moved along to keep up with styling trends. Suzuki elected to keep a familial stacked-headlight look rather than trying dual "cat eye" lights.

LEFT: Racing is more than the lifeblood of the GSX-R; it's a crucial link in the development chain. Here, Frankie Chili on the Alstare Corona GSX-R750 leads the pack during the 2000 World Superbike season. Lessons learned from competition—500 GP, MotoGP, AMA Superbike, World Superbike, and World Endurance, to name just a few of the categories in which Suzuki has competed—inform the street bikes utterly.

OPPOSITE: At the Hamamatsu engine-assembly plant, first-generation GSX-R engines were built largely by hand. Today there is more automation, but the philosophy of maximizing engineering resources and parts commonality that governed the manufacturing efficiencies at Suzuki remain unchanged.

BELOW: GSX-Rs rolled down the Toyokawa line at a rate considerably slower than today. In 1985, the hard-core repli-racer craze had only just begun, thanks to this motorcycle. Over time, the GSX-R would buoy Suzuki's sales and profitability through all kinds of world economies.

viewed for this book—at the headquarters in Hamamatsu, the Ryuyo course, the factory in nearby Toyokawa, and the U.S. subsidiary in California, American Suzuki Motor Corporation—spoke reverently about the GSX-R and what it means not just to the company but to motorcycling as a whole. Well beyond portraying the company line, they explained how the success of this motorcycle—on the road and in racing—raised the profile of the company and gave it the resources to fight larger battles and, in essence, to punch above its weight. Their tales included recollections of debates—many quite heated—about the direction of development and how best to serve the GSX-R's mounting reputation. Spend a few minutes with any of them, and you'll soon see the passion and conviction hiding just below the surface of a guarded expression.

This is a company of enthusiasts.

Good thing, because the GSX-R deserves nothing less.

18L
平野　工業

SUZUKI
HYPER SPORTS
GSX R 750

CHAPTER 2

WHERE LIGHT MET RIGHT . . .

Generation 1: 1985–1987

OPPOSITE: When the GSX-R arrived, it was a clear step ahead of the competition. It remained true to the racetrack credo—if it doesn't make it go, it doesn't belong on the bike—while displaying a unique style.

BELOW: In January 2005, Mr. Yokouchi lists the performance parameters and goals for the GSX-R on the whiteboard as he describes that period of furious development in the early '80s. His passion for excellence in engineering and maintaining low weight for maximum performance is undiminished and, more than ever, is reflected by the engineers and styling designers who are producing the current GSX-Rs.

Etsuo Yokouchi, probably in his sixties but as vigorous as any man in Hamamatsu, sits down across from the Americans in an austere conference room at the Suzuki headquarters to talk about the motorcycle that changed the world. A live wire of a man, his hands are always moving. Equal parts of his lecture on the genesis of the GSX-R—and lecture is probably not the best term, *sermon* is more like it—have him writing furiously on a whiteboard and sitting across the table, teetering on the edge of his chair, elbows forward, his gaze absolutely captivating.

Custom dictates orderly proceedings: ask the question, receive an answer. At the beginning of the interview Mr. Yokouchi sits down—barely—hands folded on a large envelope containing rare photos of the period, and says, "Shall we begin?" But before the translator can form the first syllable of the first question, Mr. Yokouchi is up at the whiteboard, scratching out graphs and specifications, comparing weights and horsepower outputs of bikes before the GSX-R.

He speaks forcefully about a story now twenty years old, a tale he has told probably a thousand times. His demeanor, his sheer enthusiasm make it seem like the first recitation—a story offered as though you were the first person kind (or perceptive) enough to ask. And he is clearly delighted to be telling it.

Inside of five minutes, you understand the nature of the man, his conviction and drive. You imagine the intense experience of the junior engineers over the years who have had to work under his exquisite dynamism. (Others later recall his passion, commenting that he has, unbelievably, mellowed with age.) He locks eyes on yours, crow's feet visible through his large glasses, until you have convinced him you understand every detail of the point he has just made. Nodding will not do. *Hai* (an emphatic "yes" in Japanese) will not do. He forces you to respond, to repeat the lesson like a first-year chemistry student. His approbation feels like a gift.

You have—you lucky soul—just met the father of the GSX-R.

Mr. Yokouchi's place in history is secure, thanks to the GSX-R. Unusual for someone in a position of power in a Japanese company, he was an outspoken critic of the way motorcycle design had taken place and an equally outspoken proponent of pushing the technology to improve the breed. Many have misunderstood the apparent lack of passion in Japanese engineers (something Mr. Yokouchi never worried about). For one thing, it's cultural; to stand proud of the company and accept credit for accomplishments can be seen as disrespectful to the rest of the team. Moreover, the culture is deeply ingrained with the concept of continual improvement. To a great degree, the people, and even the company, are of secondary importance to the product.

In late 1981 and early 1982, racing was on Mr. Yokouchi's mind; it was an endeavor he viewed as the ultimate test. "Racing is love," he says, meaning that it takes you to extremes. If a machine is to be competitive, it must be a better performer; there are no market surveys at the checkered flag, no success comes from playing it safe. Racing machines must be powerful, of course, but it is equally important that they be light and nimble. With this idea percolating in his head, Mr. Yokouchi surveyed the sportbike landscape of the late 1970s and early 1980s and plotted his course.

We look at that period from modern times and see the goal the GSX-R represented as such a clear target—reduce the weight, and even if you don't dramatically increase horsepower, performance will increase. It helps to understand motorcycling in that period to fully appreciate the impact of the first GSX-R. In the years closing out the 1970s, most sportbikes were simple derivatives of so-called standard bikes. From Japan, they were almost universally inline four-cylinder,

BELOW LEFT: The profile of all sportbikes to come: the original edition 1985 GSX-R750. Truly based on race bike technology, it pioneered the racer-replica concept for the rest of the industry. To today's rider twenty years later, this category is so familiar that it is hard to fully appreciate how revolutionary the idea was in the early '80s.

BELOW RIGHT: Sadayuki Inobe was in charge of overall engineering during the GSX-R's gestation and continues as a managing director at Suzuki. Longevity is not an unusual trait for engineers working on the GSX-R project, and many key engineers who are in management positions today were deeply involved in the GSX-R's early development.

LEFT: Suzuki developed many of the GSX-R's components on the racetrack. The GS1000R was a test bed for a lot of new technologies earmarked for the planned GSX-R, not just for the alloy frame. Its wheelbase was impressively short to improve its handling quickness, and its weight was reduced wherever possible. At the time it was not so important for endurance bikes to be light, but the combination worked well. This is the second Suzuki France endurance racer for 1983, ridden by French teammates Pierre Etienne Samin and Dominique Pernet. It placed fifth in the race. **BELOW:** Mr. Yokouchi, on the right with the garden hose, proves the theory that the oil-cooling portion of the GSX-R engine design can flow enough fluid to carry away destructive heat. The rate of oil flow and the position of the cooling nozzles—both in the head and under the pistons—were critical to breaking the oil's boundary layer for optimum heat transfer. Mr. Yokouchi had to prove the theory once again to the Japanese Ministry of Transport, which did not have a classification for oil cooling. It did when he was done.

RIGHT: The early GS1000R endurance racer at Paul Ricard also used a steel-tube frame before Suzuki began experimenting with the alloy frame. Note, however, that it already had the aluminum swingarm and the bellcrank-style Full Floater single-shock rear suspension. Also fitted is a fully machined fork with leading-caliper brakes and early antidive hydraulics.

air-cooled engines strapped to simple, round-steel-tube, double-cradle frames. This was so much the orthodoxy that a term emerged: UJM. Universal Japanese motorcycle. Despite the jingoistic ring, it was not used specifically as a damning term except by those with allegiances to other brands or continents. In fact, UJM came to mean universally good, if conservative, engineering. The bikes all started on the first try, didn't leak oil, and were typically well enough developed that they didn't shake themselves apart. The Japanese companies had many of the same resources available, and their engineers had followed many of the same paths, resulting in their bikes looking and working much alike. There was also, undeniably, some copying, the inevitable "Hey, that's a good idea ... should have thought of that."

This also was a period of transition from two-stroke to four-stroke power plants. Honda unquestionably landed the first punch with the CB750 in 1969. It reset the standards of fit and finish, durability, and broad appeal even if it was a conservative choice. Enthusiasts were lining up for crazy-fast bikes like Kawasaki's two-stroke triples. Within this category, Suzuki moved slowly. Its premier two-stroke bikes—the air-cooled GT380 and GT500, and the liquid-cooled GT750—were genuinely middle-of-the-road models. They were two-stroke versions of the CB750 in many respects.

By the late 1970s, regulations were making the two-strokes harder to get into certain markets that

had set more rigorous emissions and noise standards. As a result, the push was on to develop four-stroke alternatives. For the most part, the other manufacturers took turns stealing the limelight from one another. In 1973 Kawasaki's 900cc Z-1 cemented the firm's reputation for building lightning-quick bikes. Honda joined with more twin-cam engines. Yamaha, still trying hard with two-strokes, nonetheless developed its own line of four-stroke bikes. Slightly late to the party after playing with rotary engines in the RE-5 and thoroughly refining two-cycle power plants, Suzuki introduced its first modern four-strokes in 1976. The GS750 four and the GS400 parallel twin were the company's first toes in the water of the modern era. Soon, a GS550 arrived. And by 1978, the company had introduced the mighty GS1000.

ABOVE LEFT: Racing has always weighed heavily in Suzuki's engineering and in its corporate thinking. Here, a GSX-R400 gets its time on the asphalt crucible. Although developing a bike for the street was—and remains—a big part of Suzuki's efforts, the track and the stopwatch provide the clearest markers of the bike's progress.

ABOVE RIGHT: The winner of the 1983 Suzuka 8 Hours was this GS1000R, campaigned by Suzuki France and ridden by Frenchman Herve Moineau and Belgian Richard Hubin. The margin of victory was only twenty seconds, but the top two motorcycles dominated the field; third place was two laps down at the conclusion.

LEFT: Side by side, the resemblance of the GS1000R and GSX-R750 is clear. Styling designer Tetsumi Ishii wanted to faithfully re-create the race bike for the street GSX-R. He did so splendidly.

For '79, Suzuki brought out the seminal GS1000S, a bike built as a replica of sorts for the machines being campaigned in Superbike racing at that time. This could also be seen as the first step toward individual sport and standard models. That is, motorcycles with clearly different intent—lower handlebars and small, wind-splitting fairings for the sport models; taller bars and no fairing for the standard models; and shaft drive with a detuned engine (for more torque) for the touring riders.

The year 1979 also brought the first L model, a cruiser-like motorcycle that was little more than a cosmetic alteration of a standard model, and the G model, a shaft-drive version of (again) a standard model with a slightly deeper seat and taller handlebars (but still no standard fairing).

Though the company was relatively new to building four-strokes, Suzuki learned quickly and developed the line with astounding rapidity. Scan the brochures from the period and you'll notice something else: Suzuki's line grew fast in terms of the number of unique models. This was the result of what had become known as the Honda-Yamaha war. In the late 1970s and early 1980s, Yamaha's market share had grown rapidly

LEFT: The GSX-R's racing debut came at Le Mans in 1985. Suzuki Endurance Racing Team (SERT) teammates Herve Moineau and Richard Hubin placed second—despite a crash for Moineau in the morning warm-up—and privateers Guy Bertin, Phillipe Gouchon, and Bernard Millet were first. Placing first and second in the motorcycle's maiden race was an auspicious debut indeed. **OPPOSITE:** The jubilant Le Mans podium ceremonies are still remembered by Suzuki's engineers today.

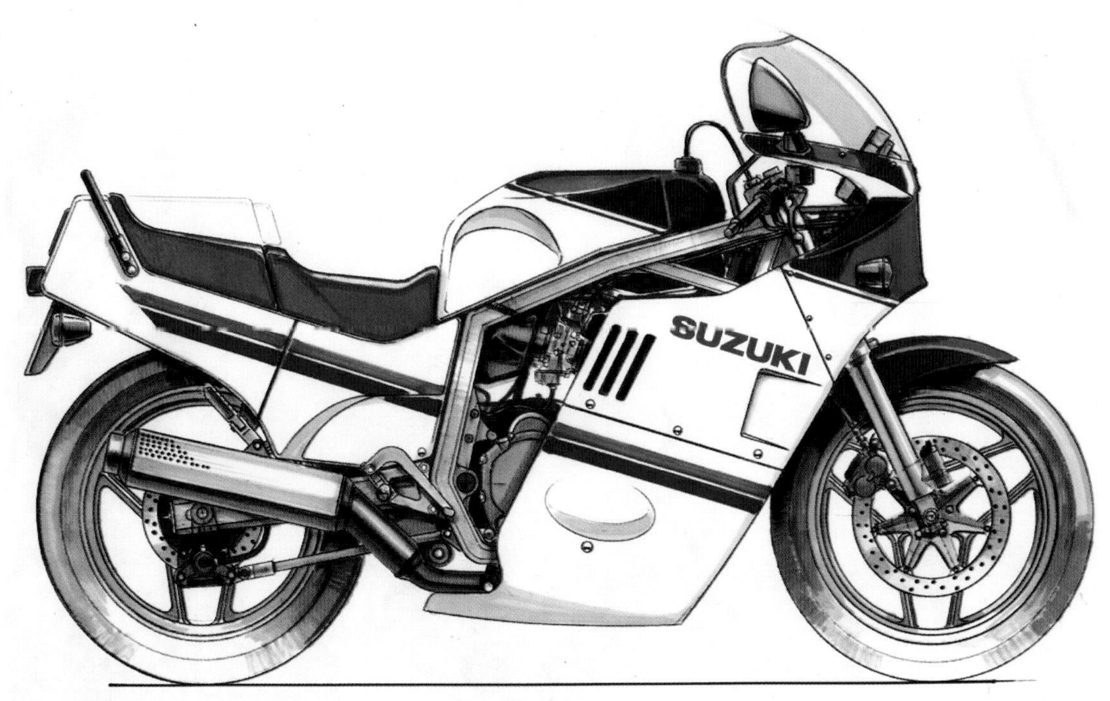

ABOVE AND RIGHT: The GS1000R's trim tail was designed with good airflow in mind. The rear pod's tight fit around the tire helped cut drag-inducing turbulence. The street-going GSX-R picked up those styling cues beautifully.

and was quickly encroaching on the perennial leader, Honda. Seeing victory within their grasp, Yamaha's managers and engineers began an all-out assault on Honda's position, building many new models, investing in technology and production equipment, and generally just ramping up as though for war. In that period, as today, Honda was much bigger than Yamaha and could increase its efforts without breaking the bank.

For companies with fewer resources than Honda and Yamaha, these were trying times. "The Honda-Yamaha war hurt us all," says Masami Haga, general manager of the motorcycle planning department. "We were forced to keep up with the new models and the advanced technology. We were carried along in the war and had difficulty surviving in it." Eventually the war ended with Yamaha calling a truce, but not until every manufacturer had been stretched to the limit developing and producing a tremendous number of models. The result was an oversupply of product placed into a softening economy. No motorcycle dealer in the U.S. at the time was particularly happy.

Even in these tough times, Suzuki continued to innovate. The company's other milestone of the period, beyond the GSX-R, was the Hans Muth-designed Katana, another model spearheaded by Mr. Yokouchi. Although its underpinnings were utterly conventional, using the air-cooled, four-valve-per-cylinder engine from the GS1100 (altered to 1000cc for the U.S. market with race homologation in mind) and an ordinary frame, its radical styling elicited gasps of surprise from

BELOW: This ghosted view shows how faithfully the bodywork follows the chassis and engine underneath. There are no swoops or styling features that are not defined by the mechanicals.

the press and enthusiasts alike. Suzuki's styling designers attempted to leverage the Katana's unusual profile into restyling jobs for other models—the GS1100E, GS550 Katana, GS650 Katana, and XN85 Turbo.

By the early 1980s, the fashion of making sportbikes separate from standards, customs, and touring rigs had fully taken hold. The engines were becoming incrementally more refined, and the chassis were starting to move toward race-like architecture, using box-section steel tubing on some models. Swingarms that had been round steel tube became gusseted steel and then aluminum. Suspension sophistication improved dramatically, as did tire construction and grip. The sport sector began to gain in sales, and the manufacturers quickly realized that a successful sportbike—particularly one that raced successfully—could benefit the entire line through raising the brand image.

In 1983, Honda introduced the VF750 Interceptor, also called V45, as in 45 cubic inches. It was, at the time, the most advanced sportbike made, and it was a model that had no direct standard-category sibling. (The VF750 Sabre, introduced a year earlier, was far removed from the V45.) This is an important distinction. Before, all manufacturers built sport models from the bones of the standard bikes. The racier version might have a bit more power, an additional brake, and possibly a lower handlebar and further rearset footpegs. Honda drove the separation of sport and standard models by allowing little of the Sabre's DNA to dilute the Interceptor's pure-sport genetics.

The Interceptor was fast and handled well but was heavier than the inline-four models it replaced. It won lots of races and more than a few awards. *Cycle Guide* magazine named it Motorcycle

LEFT: Masami Haga, general manager of the motorcycle planning department, explains the GSX-R's position within the company and among sporting motorcycles from around the world: at the top. It was Mr. Haga's belief—shared by the engineers of the time—that all-out performance was the way forward. While the rest of the industry focused on all-around competency, Suzuki pushed the GSX-R to the forefront by emphasizing pure performance.

BELOW LEFT: The Team Titan Suzuki squad races at Suzuka in 1984. The endurance racer, which also was worked into a TT-F1 machine, placed fifteenth that year with riders Hisashi Yamana and Toshiaki Hakamada. Team Titan was an integral part of testing and developing the GSX-R's engine and other components.

BELOW RIGHT: Graeme Crosby and Len Willings partnered on the Yoshimura-prepared GSX750R—the precursor to the GSX-R—at the Suzuka 8 Hours in 1984.

ABOVE: Graeme Crosby aboard the GS750E at Daytona. Notice the beginnings of a fairing that was created as part of the required number plate. At the time, factories were still thinking more about street bike suitability for their motorcycles (and thus sales) rather than pure racing potential. That would soon change.

RIGHT: Just as the GSX-R750 enjoyed a significant weight advantage over its rivals, so too did the 1100. Compared to the Kawasaki Ninja 900R—a bike considered a lightweight in the class—the GSX-R was 60 pounds lighter. It was an amazing 107 pounds lighter than a Honda VF1000R, according to *Cycle* magazine.

of the Year and chromed one to put on the cover. (That particular bike was actually a nonrunning early prototype.) At the time, the motorcycle press openly speculated that the future of sportbiking would follow the Interceptor lead without question: the bikes would become ever more sophisticated and feature driven, with the lure of new configurations—particularly the V-4—counting for a lot when it came to attracting customers.

The same was happening over at Kawasaki, as its GPz series grew in performance and weight. Even the Ninja 900R, when it appeared in 1984, was a heavy motorcycle whose powerful engine largely overcame the fact that the steel-tube chassis wasn't quite as competent as the Honda's.

Still following the traditional routes in the early 1980s, Suzuki was producing new versions of its main models, introducing air-cooled engines that were far more modern and compact than the old (but still popular) two- and four-valve engines. (The roller-bearing-crank GS1100 engine, as locomotive-like and loved as it was, nevertheless was a massive, heavy power plant.)

It was a matter of timing. Suzuki elected to take a conservative approach to the sporting philosophy, choosing to develop a bike with good sporting credentials that was also reasonably comfortable and flexible. Honda and Kawasaki went the other way, producing ever more serious-minded sportbikes, with Yamaha not far behind. History shows that the interim motorcycles weren't a great success, even as the air-cooled GS1150 forged on, still selling reasonably well. (That's a relative term. By 1984 and 1985, motorcycle sales were hurting in the U.S.)

Still, in the early 1980s, even as sportbike technology seemed to accelerate, in truth the models from every manufacturer progressed gradually in terms of technology and performance. As they took small steps up in many categories at the same time—engine power, chassis rigidity, braking performance—they also put on weight. Honda's Interceptor weighed more than 500 pounds dry, and the air-cooled Kawasaki GPz750 was just a few pounds lighter.

ABOVE: Hironori Iguchi was the engineer in charge of all of the engine's moving parts during the GSX-R development and is now senior general manager of Suzuki's board. "We were told to make it as light as possible. We have very aggressive design schemes, so it broke very often," he recalls of the extensive testing phase.

Meanwhile, back in Mr. Yokouchi's lair in 1983, domestic-market customers caught a glimpse of Suzuki's technology to come in the RG250 Gamma. It was light, very light, but you'd expect that of a two-stroke. Next, in 1984, came the GSX-R400. Think of it as the trial balloon, a relatively low-risk peek at what could be done. The engine, a liquid-cooled inline-four, was placed into an all-aluminum frame. As a result of the frame and an abnormal obsession with detail weight reduction, the little bike came in 18 percent lighter than its Japanese-market competition. It was heralded as one of the best sportbikes of the time. No doubt the other three of the Big Four were eyeing the new-think motorcycle with concern. Even if they took it seriously right from the start, they would

LEFT AND RIGHT: Racing improves the breed by removing what is unnecessary and focusing on what is critical. In high-speed competition, aerodynamics is a top priority. The GS1000R (right) had winglets molded into the fairing to smooth airflow around the rider's tucked-in hands and elbows. The GSX-R750 (left) picked up these cues but in a downsized form that was more aesthetically pleasing and better suited for a street bike.

RIGHT: By today's measure, the 1985 GSX-R750 seems tall and skinny, but this was the stuff of pure, unalloyed boyhood dreams twenty years ago. Every racing enthusiast worthy of the name lusted after one.

begin a retaliation already behind schedule.

"I felt that if we could do a 400cc bike that was 18 percent lighter, we should be able to do the same with a 750," recalls Mr. Yokouchi. It was an audacious assumption; as engineers will tell you, scaling effects are hard to predict. The critical task would be to keep everything in balance, to make every part as light as possible.

"I knew that light was the right direction," he says. "We had a voluntary 100PS [the metric equivalent of 98.6 hp] limit. We were getting close to having 100PS already, so the only avenue open for better performance was to reduce weight."

Mr. Yokouchi pushed his team relentlessly. "I asked the engineering team to bring in a GS750E4 [the 1984 air-cooled GS750E in the U.S. market] and take it completely apart. I had them paint components that we had no trouble with—no breakage or durability issues—in blue. I had them paint parts that had broken in the field in red. When we brought all the parts together, they were almost all blue! We were building the bike too well; nothing ever broke. As an engineer, I say this is wasteful. We have become too conservative." His story is corroborated by Hironori Iguchi, the engineer in charge of all the engine's moving parts during GSX-R development: "We were building very conservative engines at the time. Nothing broke."

Emboldened, Mr. Yokouchi set the goal: 100PS from a 750cc engine and 20 percent less weight than the bikes of the day, which were all around 480 pounds (220kg). Thus, the target was 379 pounds (176kg). The race was on.

Chassis development took place simultaneously with engine development, with each department charged to reduce weight wherever possible. And if such weight-saving measures called for unusual or expensive materials, new technologies would be developed to produce them economically. Suzuki was a small company at the time and simply could not afford to produce a motorcycle at a loss, no matter how important it might be to the long-term health of the company.

Mr. Yokouchi was convinced that race bike dimensions would translate to the street. "The motorcycle doesn't know where it is being ridden," he says. In other words, good handling on the track would make for good handling on the street. (In retrospect, Mr. Yokouchi and his team overstepped this idea ever so slightly, as a lengthening of the wheelbase for the 1986 model attested. Still, you have to admire his clarity of vision and willingness to stay the course.)

Suzuki had campaigned and won on the GS1000R endurance racer. It had won the Suzuka 8 Hour with riders Herve Moineau and Richard Hubin en route to winning the 1983 Endurance

BELOW: The central idea in getting oil cooling to work properly is to force it onto the surface with sufficient energy to break through the boundary layer—that area where the oil movement tends to slow and heat builds up—and to keep it moving in sufficient quantity to move the heat out of the engine through an extra-large oil cooler. The drainback tubes highlighted in the front of the engine help keep the oil moving rapidly back to the extra-large sump.

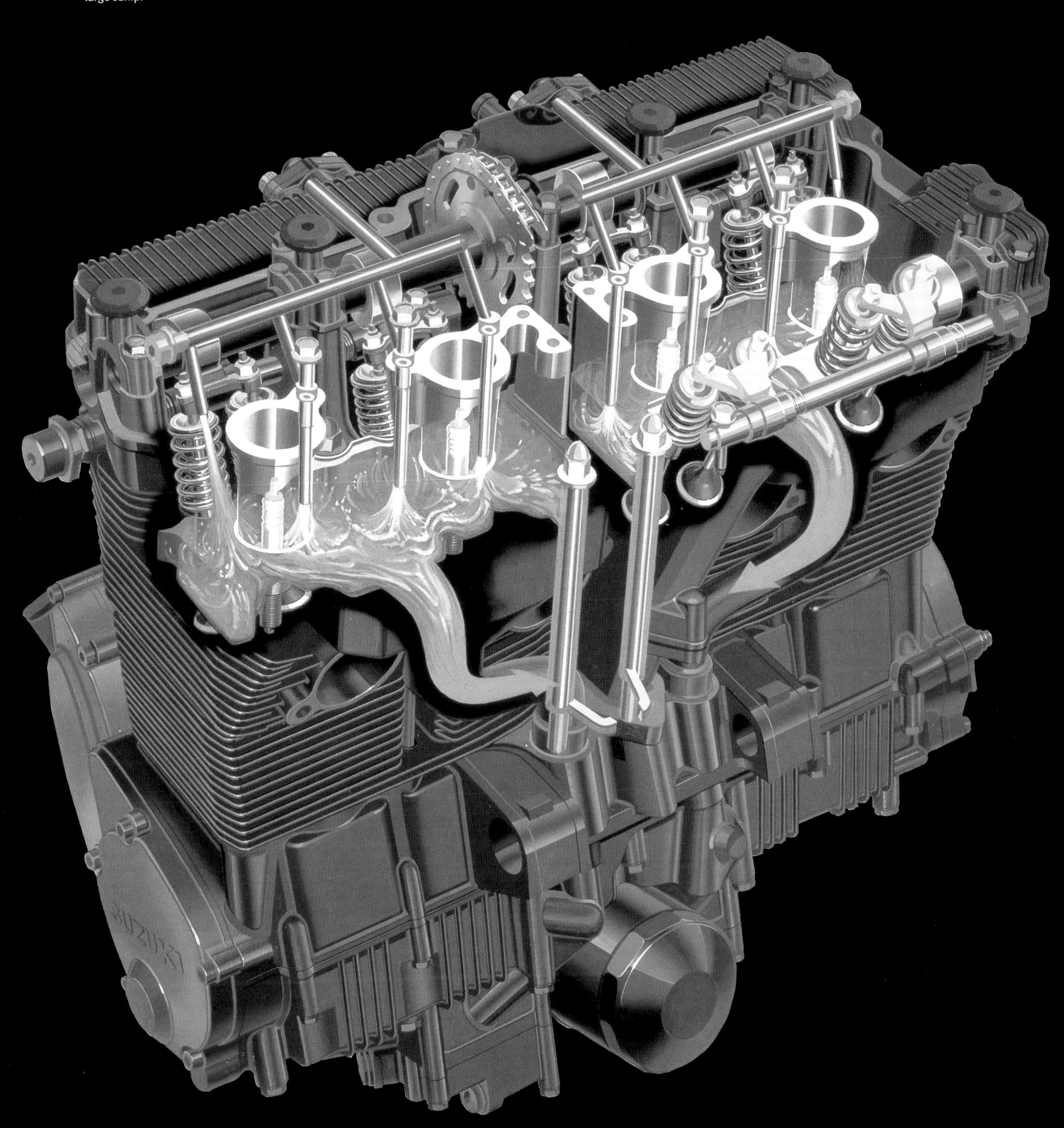

ABOVE LEFT: The first-year GSX-Rs had surprisingly comfortable two-piece seats. In the second year, Suzuki changed to a single seat with a plastic cowl to give a racing solo-seat look. **BELOW LEFT:** Teardrop-shaped mirrors show an uncommon attention to detail for the period, when many bikes had what seemed like tacked-on mirrors, lights, and turn signals. Considering that this was a racing-derived bike that was supposedly receiving these street-going pieces reluctantly, they were nicely styled and integrated.

TOP: Twenty years after the fact, how many sportbikes still look purposeful, lean, and serious? The GSX-R hit all the critical points: unique profile, unquestioned intent, superb execution. **ABOVE:** How serious was this? Race-style instruments held into a foam surround did not just give the impression of lightness but were, amazingly, actually light. The tachometer that starts at 3,000 rpm was seen by enthusiasts as a wonderfully brash signal of the bike's sporting intent. **RIGHT:** The GSX-R's dual headlights are more than a nod to the endurance racer. Law at the time required symmetrical headlights, so it was either abandon the asymmetrical layout used by the racers for a single middle beam or go with this look. It would later be emulated by every one of Suzuki's competitors.

LEFT: Naturally, track testing has always been part of the GSX-R methodology. Much of what made the bike so dominant was developed over miles and miles of riding on the test track at Ryuyo and making adjustments.

World Championship for the HB Suzuki team. Although its GS1000-derived engine was primarily air cooled, it did employ a version of oil jets aimed at the undersides of the pistons, as used on the production XN85 Turbo. The chassis was forward looking. It used a short wheelbase, tight rake, comparatively little trail, 18-inch slicks, and, most important, an aluminum-tube construction that foretold the development of the GSX-R. These tubes were a combination of rectangular and round stock welded together in true one-off fashion. But while the material was new, the overall concept was not. The frame formed a conventional double cradle, with massive main struts leading back from the steering head toward a point just aft and above the carburetors. This part of the frame then turned down to meet the swingarm pivot. Dual frame members rode down from the steering head, under the engine, and met up with the swingarm-pivot section from below. The upper tubes were moved outboard from the conventional location—steel-tube frames of this period had their main member or members close to the centerline of the bike, with the horseshoe-shaped lower part of the fuel tank draping over. Widening the upper frame members increased rigidity without having a big impact on weight, but new ways of manufacturing and mounting fuel tanks had to be considered. Plus, room for a large airbox behind the bulky engine had to be in the plan as well.

Little did competitors or race fans appreciate that they were seeing a configuration that would become synonymous with sportbike performance. And while a great deal of the GS1000R's success can be laid at the feet of its stout engine and well-organized team, the low weight afforded by the alloy frame should not be underestimated. A lighter bike is easier on its tires and on the rider, which is of particularly high importance in endurance racing.

"It was an amazing time," says Akimasa Hatanaka, part of the GSX-R chassis-design team. "We had a lot of heated discussions. How should we weld the frame? What materials are best? In a lot of ways, we were groping in the dark. But we had the racing experience to lead us. We knew that following what worked in racing would help."

The team did more than just follow; they quite faithfully reproduced the GS1000R in the new GSX-R. Rake was a dramatically steep 26 degrees, trail was 4.2 inches, and the wheelbase was a terrifically short 56.1 inches. Put in perspective, Honda's V45 Interceptor had a rake of 28.2 degrees, 3.8 inches of trail (not an unusually small number, thanks to the 16-inch front wheel), and a wheelbase of 58.9 inches. The GSX-R's dimensions weren't just smaller than the others'—they were *tiny*.

Suzuki had made other aluminum-frame street bikes before—the GSX-R400 and the RG250 Gamma two-stroke—and had worked hard to hone the material into something that could be produced within cost and time guidelines. With these requirements in mind Mr. Yokouchi's team had elected to make the frame from a combination of materials. The headstock and swingarm-pivot area are both castings. Aluminum castings can take fairly complicated shapes easily and, if made properly, require a minimum of machining and preparation before assembly. Between the cast pieces were extruded-aluminum, box-section tubes. Where the tubing runs are relatively straight and uncomplicated, extrusions offer a high strength-to-weight ratio; the key is to use each material where it is best. Moreover, Suzuki had developed an aluminum alloy that did not need to be heat treated after welding, which saved production costs. Advances in materials also led Suzuki to use lightweight cast wheels.

Mr. Iguchi recalls: "We built a boldly lightweight frame. We were pushing ourselves very hard."

BELOW LEFT: Suzuki's second motorcycle with an alloy frame was the domestic (Japanese) market GSX-R400. This liquid-cooled, inline-four-powered mighty mite was quick, handled beautifully, and made many riders utterly fearless. Suzuki noted the acceptance of this serious Supersport in planning its next move.

BELOW RIGHT: This is the profile that put the fear into the other manufacturers in 1985. Although some of the marketing managers at competing companies may not have appreciated the impact of the GSX-R—at least not right away—their engineers knew at once that Suzuki's bike would be formidable.

ABOVE: Suzuki's first street bike to use alloy chassis, square-tube architecture was the 1983 RG250 Gamma, sold in Japan. It was 18 percent lighter than its competition and became an instant sales success.

With the GSX-R, Suzuki showed its willingness to reinvent even proprietary technologies in the pursuit of reduced weight. An example is the GSX-R's Full Floater rear suspension. Previous examples of the system for street bikes used a pair of vertical struts rising from the swingarm that connected to a rocker arm. The fulcrum of the rocker arm bolted to the frame, while the free end compressed the top of the shock. The bottom of the shock was connected directly to the swingarm. But with the GSX-R, Suzuki recast the idea, solidly mounting the top of the shock to the frame. Below the swingarm is a banana-shaped linkage housing an eccentric cam that, along with the natural changes in the linkage ratio through suspension travel, made the system fairly progressive.

The reason for the change? Weight, for one, but it also lowered the overall center of gravity. Mr. Yokouchi anticipated that his new engine design might be more top-heavy than the previous generation's power plant, and he wanted to compensate. Moreover, the simplified system created room for the battery and electrical components.

The fork was also comparatively beefy. The Showa unit had 41mm tubes, where the de facto industry standard was a 39mm unit. A fad of the time was some form of antidive damping; the Suzuki had a simple rate-sensitive mechanism on the leading edge of the fork leg. This system did not reduce braking feel, and a similar one, electrically activated by the brake light circuit, would later be used on the GSX-R1100.

Eighteen-inch wheels were fitted front and rear and given either Bridgestone or Dunlop radial tires. The sizes—110/80VR18 front and 140/70VR18 rear—seem impossibly small by today's standards, but they were cutting-edge stuff in 1985. Many have asked why Suzuki did not use the then-popular 16-inch front wheel on the GSX-R. There are three answers: One, the 18-incher followed the GS1000R race bike pattern. Two, the bike was expected to be very light and therefore maneuverable. The lighter steering response of the 16-inch tire was not necessary. Third, the taller tire permitted slightly larger brakes and rotors than would be possible on a 16.

This groundbreaking chassis would carry an equally groundbreaking engine. Suzuki had done V-4 engines in the Cavalcade touring bike and the Madura cruisers, but such a layout wasn't even considered for the GSX-R. Market research and basic packaging demands pointed to the inline-four.

The turning point for the GSX-R project actually took place two years earlier, as Mr. Yokouchi and his engineering staff were trying to lower temperatures in the XN85, Suzuki's sole turbocharged motorcycle. The two-valve, air-cooled 650 engine was having trouble staying together under the kind of turbo boost that would create reasonable power. Mr. Yokouchi looked to aircraft engines for a solution. Many of the large-piston engines developed during World War II relied upon a generous amount of oil used for cooling; many radial-engine aircraft had dipsticks calibrated by the gallon rather than by the quart. Many used oil squirted at the pistons from underneath to remove some of the combustion heat. When the pistons are large, as they were in these massive radials, heat conduction to the bore is a problem. In addition, these engines were turbocharged and ran on a tremendous amount of boost, further raising combustion pressures and temperatures. The oil effectively improved the life of the engine and, in turn, allowed them to make more power without additional displacement.

Mr. Yokouchi turned to oil jets for the XN85, and they worked. File that away for future reference.

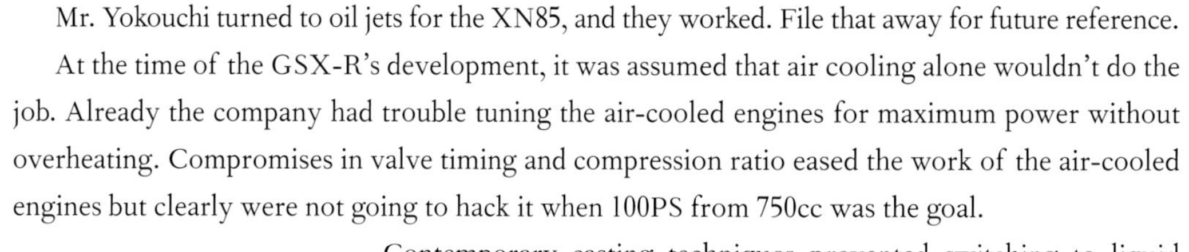

At the time of the GSX-R's development, it was assumed that air cooling alone wouldn't do the job. Already the company had trouble tuning the air-cooled engines for maximum power without overheating. Compromises in valve timing and compression ratio eased the work of the air-cooled engines but clearly were not going to hack it when 100PS from 750cc was the goal.

BELOW: The Yoshimura GSX-R appeared stock from a few feet back, but the rules at the time permitted strategic strengthening of the frame, which the Yosh team did. The geometry remained as stock, but the frame was much stronger and more stable.

Contemporary casting techniques prevented switching to liquid cooling while still maintaining the low-calorie diet. So the idea of making oil do more work was floated. This is the original story that has been circulated for the past twenty years, the linchpin to the GSX-R's success. Hemmed in on one side by the desire for horsepower that an air-cooled engine could not generate reliably and on the other side by production limitations that would have forced extra weight on the machine, Mr. Yokouchi kept thinking. In fact, he had three rules for his engineers (four if you count never sleeping): One, don't copy. Do your own thing; forget what the competition is doing. Two, go for new technology. It might be harder in the beginning, but it pays off very quickly. Three, avoid conventional wisdom. The last is probably the most persuasive. After all, the conventional wisdom of the day was that you could not build a durable, street-legal bike the weight of the GSX-R.

Oil would carry the load, so to speak. And while most refer to the GSX-R engine as being oil cooled, it's worth remembering that it's still largely air cooled. Think of the oil system as a necessary supplement, a way of getting heat out of places that vexed air-cooled engines' designers, namely, the top of the combustion chamber. Not wanting to deprive the engine of oil for lubricating purposes, a double-chamber pump was designed. The high-pressure side fed the bearings and

LEFT: Endurance racing, such as here at Suzuka, was incredibly popular in Japan and Europe during the 1980s. Suzuki believed that racing in this form, where a balance of speed and durability had to be met, was among the most demanding in motorcycling. **BELOW:** In Daytona, Wes Cooley started coming to grips with the new GSX-R after riding the GS700E—the sleeved-down version of the GS750E—the previous year.

ABOVE: Satoshi Tsujimoto's TT-F1 champion bike was based on the GSX-R but was heavily modified. Mr. Tsujimoto was revered by fans and Suzuki alike for his fearsome race craft, in much the same way that Suzuki came to admire Kevin Schwantz's overwhelming will to win. **ABOVE RIGHT:** On the Ryuyo course, the new-for-'86 GSX-R1100 was developed to be as light—comparatively—as the 750 yet awesomely fast. The 750 was considered quite quick for the day—even if its powerband was tilted toward the top end of the rev range—but the 1100 was renowned as a torquer, able to peel rubber off the rear tire at will. **BELOW RIGHT:** Mr. Yokouchi (center) celebrates victory at the Austria 6 Hours race in 1985.

RIGHT: Fujio Yoshimura, son of Hideo "Pops" Yoshimura, took over the family business in Japan. On the eve of the GSX-R's twentieth birthday, he recalls the development of the GSX-R as a racing platform. "We made big improvements over the old air-cooled bikes. The GSX-R was a race bike from the start and that helped us a lot."

BELOW LEFT: Hideo "Pops" Yoshimura began with a small racing squad that would grow into a dynasty, carried on by his son, Fujio. Mr. Yoshimura knew how to get the most out of his machines and fully appreciated Mr. Yokouchi's penchant for reducing weight and complexity. Yoshimura's race bikes were a further expression of this philosophy.

BELOW RIGHT: Meanwhile, on the four-stroke side, Suzuki was developing a new line of air-cooled motorcycles that represented incremental improvements informed by some of the engineering approaches that were planned for the GSX-R: slightly smaller engines and square-tube steel frames.

the piston-squirt jets; a low-pressure (and therefore high-volume) side fed the cooling circuit. The engine oil was, obviously, shared between these two circuits. Just to hedge bets, the engine carried 5.3 quarts (5 liters) of oil in a wet sump.

It was also assumed that the new engine would have four valves per cylinder. It was the new standard—excepting Yamaha's insistence on five per jug, a technology that debuted the same year as the GSX-R—and the right way to go for the power goals. But air-cooled engines need as much finning around the spark plug and valves as possible; the more valves, the less area for such finning.

The solution was to completely rethink cylinder-head architecture. Instead of having multiple fins across the top of the head, the head was cast as a flat plate with tall tunnels for the spark plugs. The valvetrain resided in a large aluminum valley, topped by a wide magnesium cover with thin, short fins. External oil lines came up the back of the cylinder block and fed spigots that shot a great volume of oil into the valvetrain cavity.

But it wasn't just a matter of filling the top of the head with oil and hoping for the best. Mr. Yokouchi explains how he arrived at that *Eureka!* moment that brought him to the next leap.

BELOW: The long-limbed Schwantz had a signature style aboard the GSX-R. No one would argue his outright speed and, later on as he honed his race craft, his ability to analyze a race while riding it.

ABOVE LEFT: Suzuki resisted the temptation to go with a 16-inch front wheel for the GSX-R, defying the trends of the day. Up to that point, street bikes typically had either the 16-incher or a 19-inch front hoop. The reason for the 18? That was the size of the GS1000R's wheel, and it reflected the race-derived technology Suzuki's engineers wanted for the new bike. **BELOW LEFT:** The unusually flat cam cover betrays the unusual cooling medium. Small-scale finning was used to improve heat conduction even on the cam cover. Suzuki engineers also explained that the gunmetal gray finish was chosen because it best rejected the heat. No thermal stone was left unturned.

TOP: Sportbikes of the period were just starting to get alloy swingarms, but few had a fully floating rear brake such as this—borrowed from dirt bike practice—that helped reduce wheel hop under hard braking. The cover on the exhaust was drilled for lightness. **ABOVE:** Stripped to the essentials. Suzuki simplified the GSX-R wherever possible in an effort to reduce weight—components were combined to minimize brackets, for example. Also, the prototypes had a shared hydraulic reservoir for the front brake and clutch to save weight. (That idea was not retained for production.) But that wasn't all. Groundbreaking new technologies were applied to the bike, from the special alloy frame to the use of radial tires. **RIGHT:** Deep-breathing engines need large airboxes, and the GSX-R had one carefully fitted into a recess at the back of the fuel tank. Before, it was expected that inline-four engines would breathe through an airbox directly behind the engine, which meant that it was ingesting air heated by the engine itself. The GSX-R iteration moved the airbox inlet up, away from that blast of heat.

ABOVE: The long straights at Ryuyo allowed Suzuki's test riders to exercise the 1100 ... and their courage. Measuring approximately two miles, the straights offered the bikes enough space to reach and maintain their top speeds.

> "I was a lazy boy ... it's true. In my home, we had a cast-iron bath heated by a wood fire underneath. My grandmother would tell me to continue to stir the water in the bath while it heated. Well, I was lazy, as I said, and didn't do that. I don't remember what I was doing, but I didn't think stirring the bath was important. But, over time, I realized that doing it my way took one or two extra pieces of wood to get the bath hot. I was amazed that my grandmother was right but, many years later, grateful because she gave me the key [to the GSX-R's cooling system]. It was boundary layer!"

Central to this design's success was his realization that a fluid flowing past a fixed object breaks into zones of flow. The flow nearest the object—in this case the cylinder head—tends to slow in what is called a boundary layer. As it slows, the rate of heat conduction is reduced. This could not be allowed. Oil by itself is approximately 10 percent less effective than water at picking up heat; it could not be left to languish.

Recalling his boyhood lesson, Mr. Yokouchi decided that the oil around the combustion chambers had to be kept moving to break up the boundary layer, therefore improving heat conduction. To that end, small baffle plates were installed adjacent to the spark plug tunnels. These kept the oil moving briskly past the hottest part of the head for maximum heat transfer.

So far so good. Lots of oil is in there, and it's routed to best effect. Now what do you do with it? It seemed straightforward to let the oil drop down the central cam-chain tunnel to the sump, but that was tested and found to be insufficient. Windage losses from the oil striking the cam-chain in the tunnel were one thing, but the oil foamed as well. (Common oil wasn't as good as it is now.)

Chiaki Hirata, one of the GSX-R engineering staff, remembers: "We continued to develop the oil-cooling system but found that at high rpm we lost oil pressure. We had used colored water to trace the flow of the oil, but then discovered that the oil falling down the cam-chain tunnel was

ABOVE: Even after changing from a two-part seat to a single element, Suzuki retained the ability to make the bike look like a *monoposto* by offering an optional seat cowl.

OPPOSITE: Kevin Schwantz and Satoshi Tsujimoto teamed up to take third at the 1986 Suzuka 8 Hours, an excellent result on a bike still undergoing development at the hands of the Yoshimura team.

foaming badly. Eventually, the oil pump could not take up the oil, and the pressure dropped."

Another creative solution: a pair of drain-back tubes were fitted to the front of the head, leading down to the sump. This cured the foaming problem, but Mr. Yokouchi had to prove that the flow worked. His test was disarmingly simple. He used one of the prototype engines with a cutaway cam cover. By means of a common water hose, he showed that the drainback tubes could handle a great deal of volume without backing up. "I remember standing outside the engineering office, showing the staff how it worked. We must have looked crazy, standing there getting our pants wet," Mr. Yokouchi recalls.

With the cooling medium decided upon, the team continued to work to get the power and to trim weight. "We were told to make it as light as possible," says Mr. Iguchi. "We were told to 'go ahead and hit the wall' and try to break the engine. Before that, the engine was made as solid and durable as possible—it didn't break very much—and the instruction was to go ahead and break it. We had very aggressive design schemes, so it broke very often."

Every component was scrutinized. Pistons, connecting rods, main bearings, crank—all came in for steely-eyed weight control. All were smaller—in some cases much smaller—than on the previous 750. Smaller bearings have less friction. According to a preview report in *Cycle World* in 1985, the diminutive bearings were responsible for a 3 hp savings at 11,000 rpm. Continue this kind of efficiency-seeking throughout the engines, and horsepower will come.

Of course, the traditional ways to acquire power also worked. The GSX-R engine had large valves, aggressive cams, large carburetors, and a free-flowing four-into-one exhaust system tuned to benefit high-rpm power. Oil cooling allowed for thin-stemmed valves with big heads, which were lighter yet flowed more. Light valves also tolerate aggressive cam timing and lots of lift.

Packaging played a role, too. The cylinder pitch was made as narrow as the engineers dared, given that the barrels were still air cooled. Fine-pitch finning was used on the head and block to facilitate cooling. Such finning increases the cooling area without dramatically increasing weight. This was another idea that Mr. Yokouchi borrowed from aircraft technology, but not before he had to convince the production department to improve the company's casting abilities so they could actually make the parts.

With the bores packed closer together, the bottom end was becoming narrower, but the placement of the alternator behind the cylinder bank was the next logical step. Other manufacturers had done this, mainly to get the alternator off the end of the crank as Suzuki had done. The main benefit to a narrow engine is that it can slide down and forward in the frame without affecting cornering

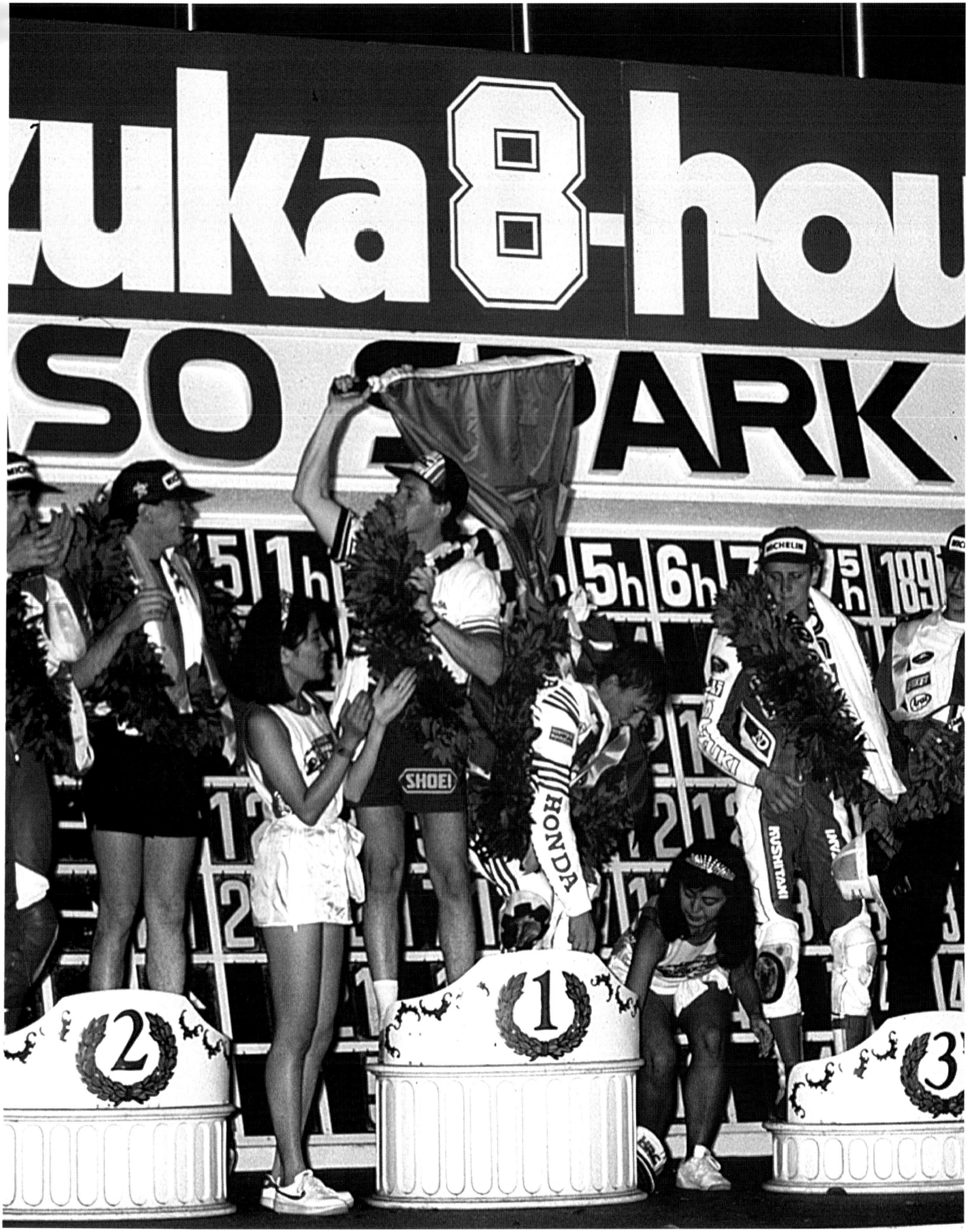

zuka 8-hou
SO SPARK
MICHELIN
SHOEI
HONDA
KUSHITANI

ABOVE: The GSX-R1100's frame was made of the same materials as the 750's frame, but it was strategically strengthened and fitted with a longer swingarm for a slightly greater wheelbase. Rake and trail numbers were slightly more relaxed, and a nonadjustable steering damper was fitted.

clearance. Look at a photo of the early 1000cc Superbikes and you'll see replacement engine covers cut at an angle to get any amount of precious clearance.

It was all coming together. "In early testing, I asked the riders and engineers to try their best to break the bike," recalls Mr. Yokouchi. "I wanted to find the weak spot. When we did find something, I had to convince them to fix only what broke. The feeling at the time was that nothing should break, so the natural reaction was to make everything heavier. But the bike has to flex if you want to keep it light."

Later, Mr. Yokouchi admitted to an American journalist that he was circumventing the normal development process, in which the race bike was derived from the street bike. "We were developing a race bike," Mr. Yokouchi said. "We had to pretend that we were making a street bike. At the end of development, we had a race bike and then had to make minimal changes to prepare it for the street." *Pretend.* No doubt if anyone could "pretend" to Suzuki management and get away with it, it was Mr. Yokouchi.

In the styling design department, there was no pretending. "There are many approaches to styling, but this is a racer replica," says Tetsumi Ishii, styling designer of the GSX-R. (In Suzuki parlance, a styling designer is responsible for the shapes and colors of the bike but is, by and large, subservient to the engineering group. It's his job to make good-looking what the engineers have determined is the right way to make the bike.) "What is most important is to keep the feeling of a racer replica," Mr. Ishii says. "I learned a lot from this project. The fairing comes from the GS1000R race bike as closely as we could. We wanted the racer look. We spent some time in the wind tunnel to determine the best shape. For example, the small wings on the fairing came directly from the GS1000R, as did the bubble windscreen."

The GSX-R's distinctive two-light face was dictated by regulation as much as by styling. "At the time, it was required that we place the headlight face at or behind the front axle," Mr. Ishii recalls. "This is why the GSX-R has this kind of face. We wanted to maintain the endurance-racer look but had to find just the right headlight to do the job and still be street legal. We could not use a single light, as on the racer, also because of the rules."

Other aspects of the bike's styling resulted from more mundane concerns. "The side panel [beneath the seat] is large because we wanted to cover the pipe hanger," Mr. Ishii says. "On the GS1000R, this was exposed, but we couldn't allow it to get in the way of the rider's feet on the GSX-R."

Also of note are the GSX-R's distinctive bullet-shaped mirrors. "We tried several designs," says Mr. Ishii. "But we came to the bullet mirrors because they worked well in the wind tunnel and were appropriate for the bike's look." Some other detailing that was picked up right from the race bike: the small vapor reservoir and external vent hose on the fuel tank, as well as the flush filler cap. In a period of design when such appurtenances would have been considered vulgar on a street bike, they were instead noticed and appreciated by enthusiasts who really wanted a "race bike with lights."

Cementing the impression was a masterstroke of design: the race-inspired instrument panel. A trio of gauges, surrounded in foam, reflected back the same image every racing enthusiast saw when peeking over the velvet rope in the pits of a GP race. The tachometer didn't even register below 3,000 rpm, just like the GS1000R. Today we might consider this an affectation, but it was meant to convey the spirit of the endeavor—to replicate, as much as possible, the race bike.

Development continued at what seems, even today, like a breakneck pace. And then it was ready.

Suzuki showed the GSX-R750 to a stunned crowd at the 1984 Cologne show, promising production for the 1985 model year. You can imagine: the carpet around the display was worn to threads. Immediately, European and domestic press were lauding Suzuki's courage in producing a full-on race bike for the streets. Enthusiasts waited as patiently as they could. And those who said, "Great, a racer for the street. It won't make a good street bike," would in many ways be proven right. But they were also to be roundly ignored by a suddenly large and vocal subset of hardcore enthusiasts for whom this was the *perfect* motorcycle.

BELOW: This was absolutely state of the art for 1985. The GSX-R used a central cam drive and a primary drive via gear mated to the number-three cylinder's right-hand crank cheek. Although the main-bearing journals and cylinder pitch look wide by today's standards, this was an incredibly compact and lightweight engine for the mid-1980s.

SUZUKI
HBSUZUKI
HBSUZUKI
MICHELIN
DECA PISTON

OPPOSITE: Tetsumi Ishii was the styling designer of the original GSX-R. "I was asked to take as much from the GS1000R racing bike as I could," he says. A quick glance at the bike from any angle shows that Mr. Ishii masterfully achieved his goal with the GSX-R.

In March 1985, *Cycle* magazine said, presciently, "Sportbikes will soon be divided into two categories: before the GSX-R, and after."

In the May 1985 issue of *Cycle*, Kevin Cameron wrote: "What Suzuki has done with every part of this machine is what has had to be done with every part of GP and endurance-racing machines several times a year, and the technique works; detailed design with critical thought to preserve or enhance function while simplifying and adding lightness. Suzuki has done more even than that—the company has brought this kind of reasoned design to the marketplace at a competitive price. And that is the best integration of design and manufacturing technology seen so far."

For the April 1985 issue of *Motorcyclist*, Jeff Karr, who attended the world press launch in Japan, reported: "The GSX-R750 put on an impressive show [at] Ryuyo. When recently shod and ridden well, it's a tremendously fast race bike, which should make it a wickedly fast bike on a racetrack-like road. Its café racer riding position will hurt it on tight roads, but the tremendous motor will let it make up a lot of ground." In concluding the story, he said, "The 750 class has gone from stale to startling this season. For now we Americans will have to be content with the [Yamaha] FZ750. Next fall the Suzuki GSX-R750 will arrive on our shores and the sporting motorcyclist will be confronted with one of the most pleasantly difficult decisions in memory."

Comments in the American press mirrored those in Europe and Canada where the GSX-R was a smash hit, as everyone had hoped. But the bike was not brought into the U.S. until 1986. Why? "We had a production limit," says Takeshi Hayasaki, group leader of the planning group for overseas marketing. "And the American market was very different, less into sport riding than in Europe.

BELOW LEFT: Crafted from a clever combination of specially extruded square members and cast pieces, the GSX-R's frame weighed only 18 pounds. It followed design convention of the time, with the integral rear frame and high-arching main members reaching well up and over the engine.

BELOW RIGHT: Here the change in frame material from the cast steering-head section to the formed main-beam extrusions can be seen. Suzuki used each material where it made the most sense, from both an engineering and a production standpoint.

ABOVE: Styles may change, but the classic two-by-two beauty shot is timeless. A performance image was pushed hard in GSX-R marketing materials, an unusual approach in a time when most manufacturers strove to produce good all-around motorcycles.

American Suzuki was concerned that they would not have as much success with the bike."

On the other side of the ocean, American Suzuki's Mel Harris explains: "In 1985 they were not sold in the U.S. That became a sore spot for our dealers, but also that time was turbulent in the industry and we had insurance problems. Part of the reason the bike didn't come here was the ITC tariff on bikes 700cc and above. We had to pay the tariff in 1986, but it wasn't as high as it would have been in 1985. The retail price with the tariff would have been too high." The so-called ITC tariff—imposed by the International Trade Commission—placed a steep financial burden on imported motorcycles of greater than 700cc. Japanese manufacturers were allowed to bring in 6,000 bikes per year on a quota system without the tariff. But the new tariff, signed into law in 1983 by President Ronald Reagan, imposed stiff sanctions on bikes 700cc and larger. The first year into law, the tariff was a staggering 49.4 percent—in subsequent years, the tariff would be reduced to 39.4 percent, 24.4 percent, 19.4 percent, and 14.4 percent, respectively. For most of the manufacturers, this rule required expensive changes to the existing 750 class machinery so they would fit under the 700cc rule. Suzuki reduced the GS750's displacement to 699cc, but never tampered with the GSX-R. The belief was that its top-line sportbike should not be emasculated and that, when finally introduced in 1986, the 24.4 percent tariff would be slightly more tolerable than the 39.4 percent tariff of the year before.

So the GSX-R—except for those bikes brought in through Canada—didn't grace American roads until 1986. By then, Suzuki had reacted to complaints of a slight lack of stability from European riders and extended the GSX-R's swingarm by a full inch.

Continues Harris: "In the second year, when we rolled them out, I think there was a lot of apprehension on everybody's part with the insurance. We were disappointed because we thought it would be a huge sales success. But it actually started slowly. At the end of the year we were wondering what we had to do. That's when we developed the GSX-R Cup, which ran out in Riverside, California, for the first time. At about that time—late in the season—it really kicked in. People realized we had a real race replica. They saw that it was everything you wanted to have if you were a motorcycle enthusiast. It took off." The GSX-R Cup was a one-make national racing series built to encourage privateers' involvement. It has since evolved to include the popular SV650 model as well.

BELOW: In the U.S., Suzuki was the first company to offer a serious full fairing on a sportbike, and the GSX-R's was by far the most radically designed from an ergonomics point of view. Another aspect of the bike drew gasps of admiration: clip-on handlebars put under the triple clamps, straight from the manufacturer ... unheard of! Previously, full fairings and handlebar assemblies such as these had been available primarily as aftermarket items from European café racer accessories companies.

Early on, there were suggestions that a bike so light could not be durable. Aiming to test the theory, *Cycle World* conducted a twenty-four-hour endurance test. It took place at Uniroyal's massive five-mile-long circular track that would allow the GSX-R to run flat-out for as long as it could. "We wanted to see just how good the GSX-R was," recalls Paul Dean, then editor of *CW* and now editorial director. "And we wanted to do the test with a stock bike." (The previous record was held by a modified motorcycle.) "We sent David Edwards [then feature editor and now editor in chief of *Cycle World*] to the Suzuki factory, where he randomly picked two bikes off the assembly line and then sealed the engines with wire and a tamper-proof seal. I had met with American Suzuki president Mr. Shigenoya, and he liked the idea. He claimed that durability of the bike would not be a concern. 'We have already run the engine at its power peak for twenty-four hours on the dyno,' he told me."

In the end, despite problems with tires chunking—a malady that Dean says he later discovered to be the result of replacement tires being put on the track without any heat cycling; the "green" tires just didn't make it—the team got its record. The quicker of the two bikes averaged 128.303 mph for the twenty-four hours, beating the old record by more than 10 mph.

Other magazines decided to test the GSX-R's mettle on the track. In a 1986 racetrack comparison by *Cycle Guide* magazine, Wes Cooley and Kenny Roberts rode the GSX-R750 and the Yamaha FZ750 against their old race bikes to illustrate how close each new production motorcycle had come to real race technol-

BELOW LEFT: Suzuki proudly displayed the fact that its new single-shock rear suspension was a derivative of its dirt-tested Full Floater technology. To reduce the overall height of the system and its weight, the normal Full Floater rocker arms and struts were replaced by an eccentric spool mounted below the swingarm to provide a progressively stiffer suspension.

BELOW RIGHT: In 1987, the Yoshimura team and Kevin Schwantz worked hard in the Daytona 200 but came up short. Victory would be achieved in a little more than three months at the Loudon round of the Superbike championship. The following year, Schwantz would win the 200 in commanding fashion, running the GSX-R's new short-stroke engine.

ogy. They discovered that the gap from racetrack to street had closed dramatically from where it had been just a few years before. The article's author, Jerry Smith, concluded, "Based on what we learned at Willow Springs, the blurring of the distinction between street bikes and race bikes is anything but sales hype.... For the next generation of high-performance street bikes, the jump from the racetrack to the street might be so short that you'll be able to smell the hot oil and hear the fans cheer every time you push the starter button."

For the first generation of GSX-Rs, Suzuki's engineering staff barely had time to draw a breath. The GSX-R1100 was ready for 1986, based strongly on the 750 but significantly altered for the crankshaft horsepower. It was scarcely heavier than the 750 and, as a result, a featherweight compared to the liter bikes in the class. To bolster its racing efforts, in 1986 Suzuki also produced a special limited edition of the GSX-R750 that sported larger brakes, a dry clutch, solo seating, and a host of other small changes.

As expected, the race bike ambitions of the GSX-R750 were played out for real. Remembers Yoshimura's Don Sakakura: "Back then, Superbike racing was based off a production bike. Suzuki would supply us with production motorcycles in the crate. They'd require extensive modifying of the chassis and the suspension, including strengthening of the chassis. Switching to the 750E4 [the GSX-R's predecessor], it was a lot easier. They were more designed for performance. The chassis didn't need all the modifications and gusseting the GS1000s did. We still had to develop our own camshafts, and we worked with Mikuni back then to develop the VM series of carburetors for racing. But the GS750 was a lot easier to work with, from a racing standpoint, than the GS1000."

Everything changed when the GSX-R750 finally arrived for stateside racing in 1986. Mr. Sakakura says: "With the GSX-R, we got the aluminum chassis and the engine performance; from that point it made our job that much easier. We didn't have to go all through it, strengthening the frame. It worked really well as a production bike for the track. Most of what we did was to make changes to make the rider comfortable rather than wholesale changes in the engine and chassis. It was just a very balanced package that worked well everywhere. The engine we continued to develop, but the chassis we left alone. It was a huge advantage."

And so it continued. While the GSX-R did not come to dominate AMA Superbike racing against the better-funded factory teams from Honda and Kawasaki, it was a complete and total sales success. Though few fully understood the impact of the GSX-R in the mid-1980s, it's clear in retrospect that it turned an industry on its ear.

Says Masaaki Kato, president of American Suzuki, "The GSX-R put Suzuki on the map."

LEFT: American Suzuki Motor Corporation President Masaaki Kato has watched the success of the GSX-R in the U.S. with keen interest. "It has always been an important motorcycle for us. It helps create our identity."

BELOW LEFT: For the last year of this generation in 1987, the GSX-R750 received only minor updates, including new paint schemes. Big news and exciting developments were just around the corner.

BELOW: Team Yoshimura manager Don Sakakura with the only figure that counts in racing: the coveted No. 1. Mr. Sakakura has presided over the development of the GSX-R as an icon in the AMA Superbike series.

SUZUKI

CHAPTER 3

RACING DRIVES DEVELOPMENT—AGAIN

Generation 2: 1988–1991

OPPOSITE: Although the engine moved to a short-stroke design and received a significantly altered cylinder head, it was fundamentally the same. It kept Mr. Yokouchi's lightweight oil-cooling system featuring dual oil pumps and a massive oil cooler. The shorter stroke permitted a higher redline and therefore better rev potential; Suzuki turned that into greater peak horsepower.

BELOW: The new 1988 GSX-R is shown at speed on the track at the company's Ryuyo test facility.

Without question the first-generation GSX-R was an out-of-the-ballpark success. The model turned the sportbiking world upside down. With one deadly accurate slash of the knife, it caused every other sportbike manufacturer to bleed sales and, once through triage, to rethink its evolutionary product-development process.

But even though the GSX-R—due credit to the 1100, but the 750 in particular—was doing extremely well in showrooms, it wasn't winning everything in sight on the racetrack. Kevin Schwantz's first season aboard the GSX-R, 1986, netted a single win in AMA Superbike. Honda's first aluminum-frame VFR750 arrived that year, and Fred Merkel put the company's substantial (some said "enormous") race budget to good use, winning his third title in a row by '86. The next year Schwantz took five wins and came home second in the championship. But it wasn't enough for Suzuki, whose corporate pride was hanging way over the line. The GSX-R was conceived to win, and win it would.

In the U.S. and abroad, the competition had stepped up to Suzuki's challenge with the GSX-R, but plans were in place to advance the state of the art. The result, which debuted as the 1988 GSX-R750J model, represented a wholesale revision of the bike, with every part of its design—engine, frame, suspension, bodywork—dramatically revised.

In modern motorcycle product-development cycles, everything is carefully considered and planned well in advance. By the time a model is introduced, the development engineers have long been hard at work on the next model, seeking to institute changes they could not make in the previous iteration and, perhaps, stamping their name on the bike itself through pet technologies. This well-ordered world had, up until the mid-1980s, worked mainly on four-year cycles. Introduce a new model, and make few changes in year two. Perhaps make small updates in year three, with cosmetics the main focus of year four. Then introduce a new model and start the process over again.

OPPOSITE: On the road and, of course, on the track, the high-winding GSX-R750 remained a formidably serious tool.

TOP LEFT: Without bodywork and ancillary parts in place, the 1988 GSX-R750 remained true to the GSX-R legacy with an over-the-top frame. However, all the important dimensions—wheelbase, rake, and trail—were reduced in an effort to make the bike more compact and better handling.

TOP RIGHT: The profile is familiar, but the frame is all new and the engine is significantly revised, though it's still based on the first-generation engine. Oil cooling featured prominently and had become a key characteristic of the GSX-R's identity, as had the perimeter frame.

BOTTOM LEFT: Fitted with the now-fashionable seat hump, the GSX-R looked even more like the racetrack refugee it was.

BOTTOM RIGHT: Suzuki entered the second generation of the GSX-R with an all-new motorcycle, not a warmed-over version of the original. It would further refine the original concept and become a stellar sales success.

But Suzuki had reset the standards with the first GSX-R and had only heightened competition. Every Suzuki engineer knows the phrase "To stand still is to fall behind." And for 1988—a year earlier than motorcycle enthusiasts and the press expected—Suzuki launched a new GSX-R750. Although it followed in the footsteps of the first version, emphasizing low weight and "hyper-sports" handling, it was as much a change from the first-gen GSX-R as the GSX-R itself was from the GS750 that had come before. In short, Suzuki left no dyno unoccupied in the search for race-winning performance. What's more, the '88 debut of the J model GSX-R750 also predicted a further shortening of the development cycles. By the time this second-generation GSX-R was done, it had seen four major revisions in as many years.

Central to the new bike was a radically short-stroke version of the oil-cooled engine. There are many ways to make more power for a given design; one is to increase the potency of the combustion event by flowing more air through the head or raising the compression ratio. But engines are a careful balance of conflicting design requirements. Raise the compression ratio and you erode detonation margins, which are thinnest when the engine is running at its hottest. Increase engine power, and it *will* run hotter. At some point, you reach the limit of the cooling system. Other methods have to be considered.

For Suzuki, that alternative was more rpm. With that goal in mind, the engineering staff shortened

the 750's stroke by 4mm and increased the bore by 3mm. A shorter stroke results in lower piston speeds so that a higher rev ceiling can be considered; for the 750 it rose to an absolutely giddy 13,000 rpm. All else being equal, if you can maintain torque output at the top of the rev band and increase the maximum, horsepower will go up.

Juggling the bore/stroke relationship sets off a series of other changes, so although the J model's engine outwardly resembles the first-generation GSX-R's, it shares remarkably few parts. The new pistons are slightly heavier than the long-stroke engine's but result in a higher compression ratio, now 10.9:1, which is fairly high for an engine of that period. They are mated to connecting rods 3.5mm shorter than the previous iteration's that, in turn, hook to a crankshaft with 2mm larger journals. Despite reduced counterweight size, the whole crank is slightly heavier than before but considerably stronger. All of these changes were made to improve the engine for racing. Indeed, Suzuki personnel admit that they might have been sacrificing roadability for racetrack success. "We wanted more high-rpm power. That was the main goal," says Chiaki Hirata, a member of the engineering team for the first generation of GSX-R engine.

To fully capitalize on the increased rpm ceiling, the new GSX-R received camshafts with more overlap and duration that open larger valves. In fact, the J model's valves are the same size as the GSX-R1100's. Feeding this reworked cylinder head were four 36mm Mikuni carburetors that introduced a new semiflat slide arrangement. To make sure they were up to the short-stroke

BELOW: From the outside, the 1988 GSX-R750 engine appeared little changed. But under the skin there was an important difference that promised more power: a radically short-stroke configuration. The stroke was 4mm shorter with a 3mm-larger bore.

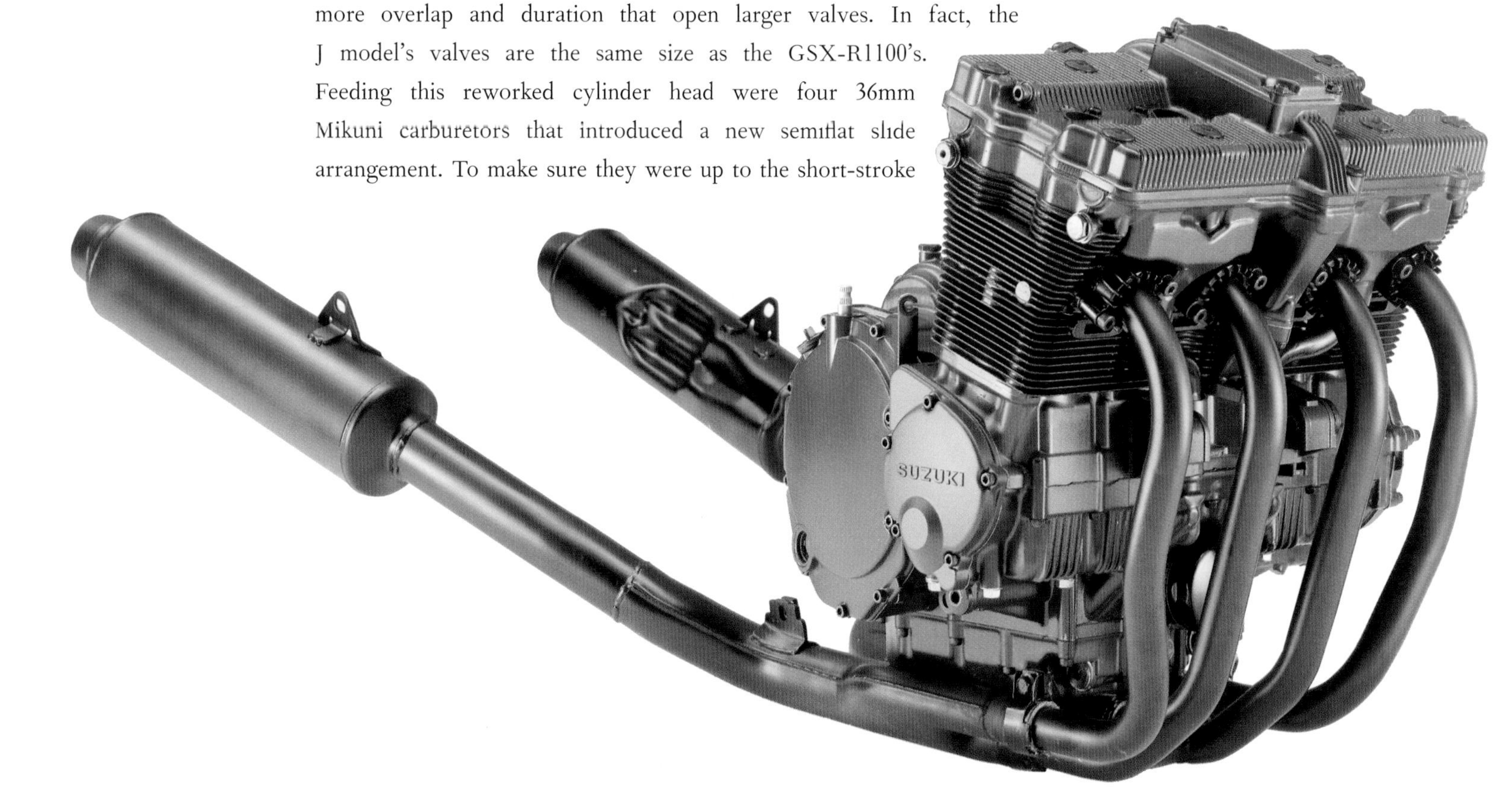

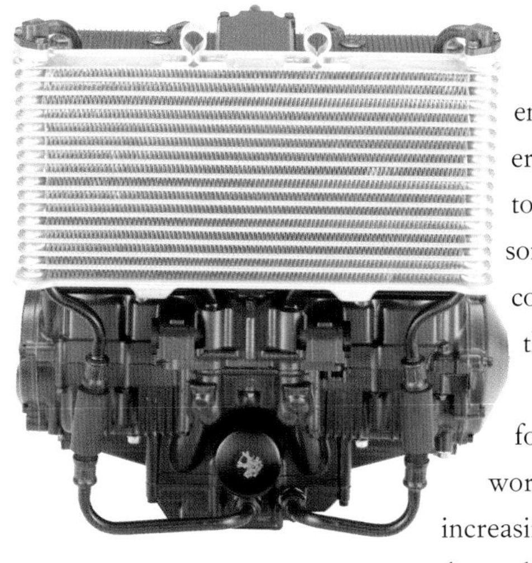

engine's airflow requirements, they were 2mm larger than the mixer on the previous engine. Because a dense air charge helps power, too, Suzuki ducted cool air from the front fairing to the airbox area; some of that air also went to the back of the engine to help keep it cool. This could be considered a nascent form of ram air, although the primary benefit was lower intake-air temperatures.

On the other end of the system, the GSX-R gained a new four-into-two exhaust system. The original GSX-R proudly wore a race-like four-into-one system with a massive muffler, but increasing noise regulations, along with the desire to increase exhaust volume, led Suzuki to go with paired mufflers. A slight weight penalty was considered worthwhile against the power increase.

LEFT: Inevitably, with more power comes additional heat. Suzuki responded by increasing the size of the oil cooler to gigantic proportions. The cooler was 17 percent larger than the preceding unit to handle greater volume.

BELOW: New styling for the second-generation model retained the familiar GSX-R look but added small ducts to the nose fairing that brought cool air to the top of the engine and to a point near the airbox. This was not true ram air because the airbox was not yet a sealed unit pressurized by the cool air being routed toward it.

Without question there was more power—contemporary magazine reports had the J model at just over 90 hp to the rear wheel, an 11 hp jump from the long-stroke 750. In fact, the 750 now made close to the same power as the GSX-R1100 (albeit without the meaty midrange torque) and vanquished everything else in the 750 class of '88, which was clustered in the 82 to 85 hp range. Most of the power advantage came at high rpm; from 9,000 rpm to the redline, the new short-stroke engine positively killed the old engine.

More power means more heat, and Suzuki continued to work the oil-cooling angle for all it was worth. (With the benefit of two decades' hindsight, we know that oil cooling would eventually reach its limit. Even the engineers admit they knew as much at the time.) The new bike carried 15 percent more oil that circulated through an oil cooler said to be 48 percent more heat efficient, and a higher-capacity pump, allied to new fittings and lines, increased overall oil flow by 20 percent. That's straightforward engineering stuff, but Mr. Yokouchi's team looked into a few other tricks to help get the heat out of the cylinder head and into the airstream. Primary among these are new baffles that fit into the recesses in the head intended to carry a large volume of oil. By adding baffle plates, the oil flow in that area must accelerate. A careful balance is at work here. Move the oil too slowly and it will readily absorb so much heat that it boils. Move it too quickly and it does not have time to absorb all the heat the cylinder head is trying to reject. In the early GSX-Rs, it was enough to let the oil do its natural thing in this area; with more power and more heat to reject, these new baffles were deemed critical.

BELOW: These GSX-Rs were commendably narrow, even though they were roughly equivalent to other bikes of the times in overall height and in the distance from the seat to the handlebars.

Suzuki enveloped this thoroughly revised engine in an entirely new frame that borrowed liberally from the company's racers of the previous year. Moreover, the new frame was designed to be strong *and* easier to produce. It didn't seem terribly important at the time, but the '88 GSX-R's frame was constructed in a way that the company would maintain until the 2005 models (and, probably, beyond.) Where the previous GSX-R frame was built of aluminum tubes and extrusions welded together, the new frame incorporated cast-aluminum sections at the steering head and swingarm pivot. These complicated shapes are much easier to create in a casting than they are with welded members.

In order to create as compact a bike as possible, the new GSX-R750 had a shorter wheelbase (by some 2 inches) at 55.1 inches, less rake (24.8 degrees vs. 26.0), and less trail (3.9 inches vs. 4.2). Where the first-gen GSX-R eschewed the trendy 16-inch front wheel, the '88 bike took a gamble with new, wider 17-inch rims, front and rear, intended to carry Michelin's just-designed low-profile radial sport tire in sizes 120/70 and 160/60. (Yes, that rear seems awfully small nearly twenty years later.)

BELOW: When Suzuki switched to the short-stroke design, the combustion chambers were altered significantly. The long-stroke engine's chambers (seen on left) housed smaller valves than the new design. The larger valves, along with the reduced average piston speeds of the short stroke, helped increase both high-rpm power and the engine's ability to rev higher.

Suspension, too, came in for a major overhaul, and it now featured a new cartridge-type fork with preload, rebound, and compression adjustments. A new, nonreservoir shock worked through a revised linkage rear suspension. In this respect, Suzuki was leading the pack by not just putting high-end technology on the street—this was among the first applications of the dirt-derived cartridge fork—but by giving the rider an unprecedented range of adjustments. Up to this point most sportbikes had suspension adjustments for spring preload in the front and preload plus rebound damping in the rear, often just four to six "clicks" of adjustment. In fact, the first road tests of the new GSX-R pointed out that it was easy to get lost in the suspension adjustments and that it was easy to make the bike handle strangely by going off on the setup.

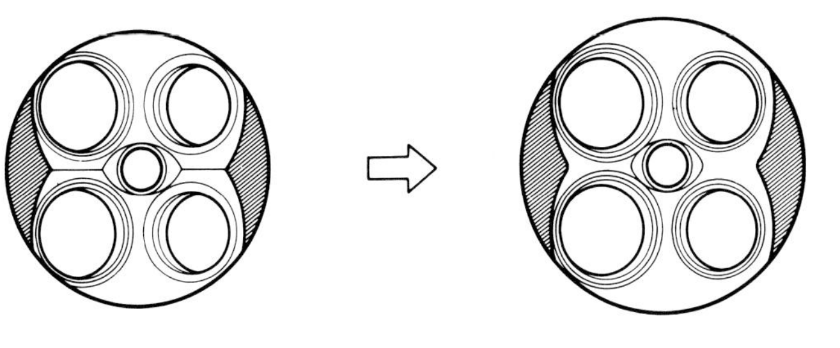

Contemporary reviews rated the short-stroke GSX-R750 high for pure performance but noted that the high-rpm-biased engine power required the utmost commitment from the rider. The exhaust system could drag in corners, but some of that might have been due to the new generation of stickier tires.

No question: the GSX-R had grown and become far more tightly focused as a result of breeding for the track. The magazines were full of praise. *Cycle*'s test resulted in this statement, "But let's get one thing straight: Serious, complex and demanding as the GSX-R is, it's best understood as a road-legal racer—a 'street bike' that's as far removed from the street as Laguna's corkscrew is from Sunset Boulevard. On this 750, straight pavement becomes almost a perversity."

LEFT: Dennis Smith is aboard the Team Hammer GSX-R1100 endurance racer. The team took the title that year and became a dominant team in American endurance racing under the leadership of John Ulrich.

RIGHT: In 1989 Scott Russell rode the 750 Supersport class at Daytona and would be an integral part of Suzuki's emergence in that category.

Once more, Suzuki took the GSX-R to the brink of what is acceptable performance for an everyday bike. But, as Sadayuki Inobe, Suzuki's current executive general manager, says, "The GSX-R has always been about 'born on the track.' That is what is important."

At the outset, the J model was intended to be a better racer, and it was. Kevin Schwantz won the AMA Superbike round at the famed Daytona 200 —and Doug Polen finished second in the series to Bubba Shobert's Honda. That same year, Suzuki won the World Endurance championship with a bike based on the GSX-R1100.

Still, the new short-stroke engine wasn't easy for the smaller teams to tune. It would take the combined talents of Yoshimura's U.S. engineers and tuners working closely with their counterparts in Japan to make the top-line bikes competitive. The smaller teams struggled as they discovered that hard-won tuning techniques from the previous engine didn't work on the revver. Suzuki, very much engineering driven and surprisingly light on hubris, immediately put together a special double-R model for 1989 that reverted to the previous "long-stroke" configuration but also came with special race bodywork and significant revisions to make the bike a true "out of the crate" racer. Just five hundred were made.

Takahiko Kawaguchi was the designer in charge of the '89 double-R model. "There are a lot of differences that aren't easy to see," he says. "For example, the fairing had to be changed to allow making it from fiberglass. The forward part was slightly longer than the regular GSX-R's for aerodynamics." And although much of what was done under the skin was dictated by engineering, there was still some leeway. "The riders wanted to be more comfortable for the track," he continues, "so we changed the shape of the side fairings and lowered the windscreen for better aerodynamics when

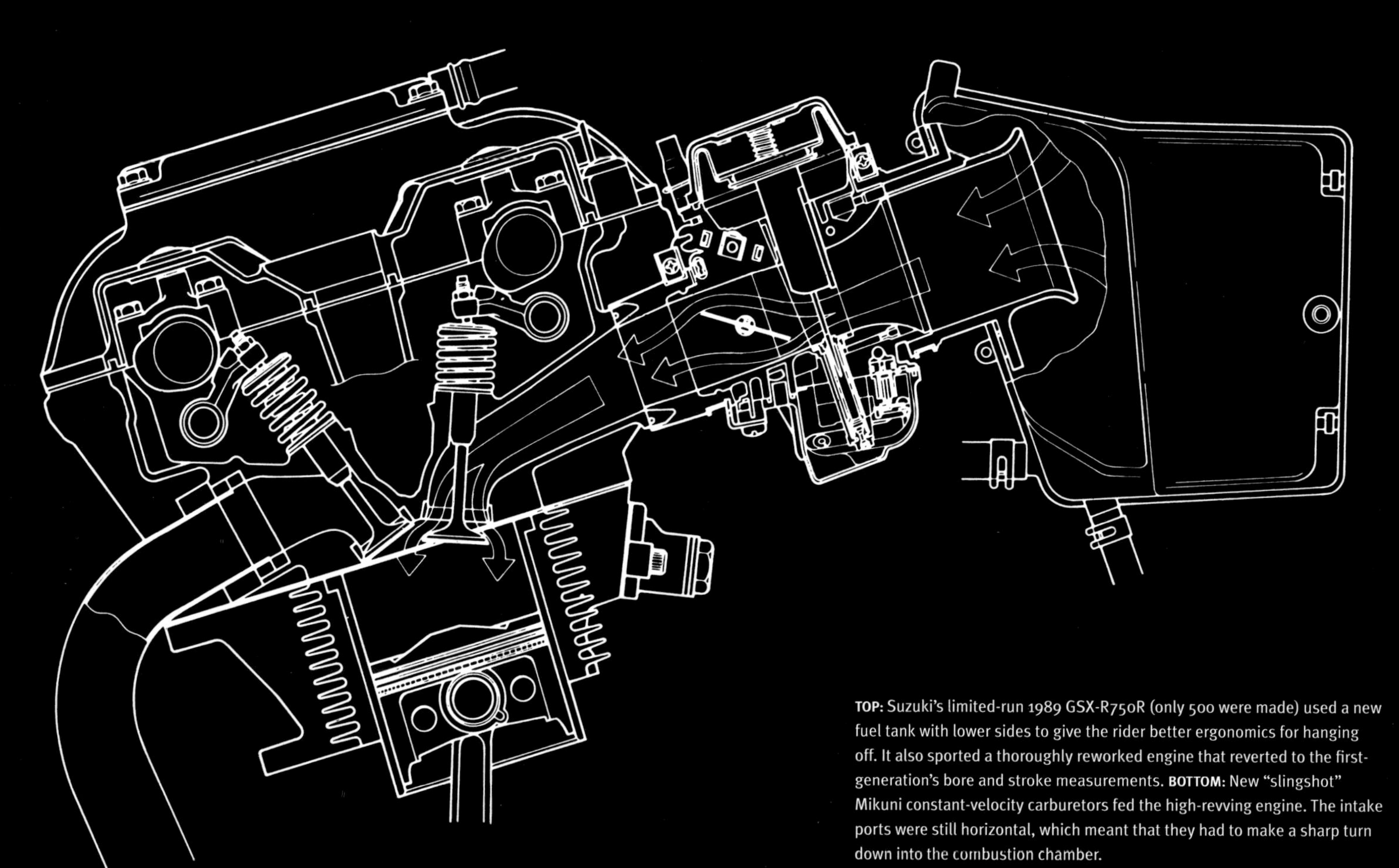

TOP: Suzuki's limited-run 1989 GSX-R750R (only 500 were made) used a new fuel tank with lower sides to give the rider better ergonomics for hanging off. It also sported a thoroughly reworked engine that reverted to the first-generation's bore and stroke measurements. **BOTTOM:** New "slingshot" Mikuni constant-velocity carburetors fed the high-revving engine. The intake ports were still horizontal, which meant that they had to make a sharp turn down into the combustion chamber.

LEFT: For this generation of the GSX-R, Suzuki switched from a four-into-one exhaust system to a system using dual mufflers, due to increasingly stringent noise-emissions regulations.

ABOVE LEFT: The head-on view of the 1989 machine is classic GSX-R, with a narrow fairing, bubble windscreen—slightly larger on the second-generation bike—and bullet mirrors. By this time the GSX-R identity had been well established among sportbike enthusiasts, and Suzuki was careful to avoid deviations from the core styling cues of such a popular bike. **ABOVE:** As had been scheduled for the 1989 model year, Suzuki updated the 1100. It received a chassis very much based on the 750, with a second-generation alloy frame and race-inspired bodywork. Though the other liter bikes of the period were getting faster, Suzuki's emphasis on lightweight design kept the 1100 among the lightest.

LEFT: Takahiko Kawaguchi was the styling designer for the 1989 limited edition GSX-R750R, a race-ready version with numerous changes to the bodywork intended to improve its competitiveness under the Superbike homologation rules. The GSX-R had begun as a street bike that reflected race bike technology; the 750R had come full circle and was a race bike issued as a street bike to compete under the existing regulations.

the rider is tucked in. We also made the front fender smaller to allow more air to the engine, and the top of the aluminum fuel tank is sloped down." This last change helped keep the rider's elbows from catching on the sharp edges of the tank cheeks.

Although only five hundred were minted, the double-R model had persuasive influence on the GSX-R line. The next year, Suzuki debuted the GSX-R750L. If you thought even a medium-size motorcycle company like Suzuki couldn't react quickly, then you would have been set straight by the '90 bike. Although it reverted to the bodywork of the standard '89 bike, the L model kept the longer-stroke version of the engine that debuted with the double-R. Mr. Hirata explains the decision, "We had tried a short-stroke 750 with the GS700E for the American market and it worked well." Still, racers, and even some street riders, were calling for more midrange torque, and Suzuki delivered.

Cycle magazine, describing the new long-stroke engine in its January 1990 issue, said: "The short-stroke engine had gone too far. With its broad, dish-shaped combustion chambers, and big inlet tracts and valves, it produced poor intake velocity and charge motion at moderate engine

MINOLTA
Castrol
SUZUKI
Castrol
MINOLTA
Castrol
NGK
MICHELIN

speeds." Some riders liked the very top-end-weighted powerband, but many found it too inaccessible for street riding. The bike that defined a race bike's personality for the street had, apparently, taken it a bit too far.

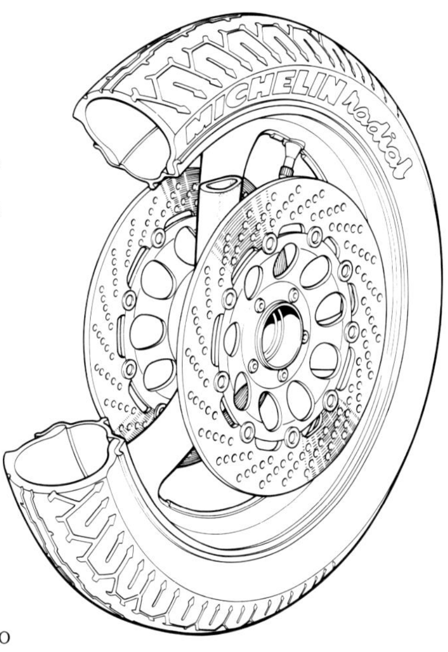

Suzuki took the opportunity to improve midrange in other ways, decreasing valve sizes slightly (by 1.3mm on the intakes and 1.0mm on the exhausts) to improve flow velocity at lower revs. The spark plug was also smaller, a 10mm unit in place of the previous 12mm, which allowed for more material between the valves. Addressing cornering-clearance complaints, Suzuki switched back to a four-into-one design with a right-hand muffler, now with a bevel along the leading edge.

Numerous seemingly small changes to the engine produced impressive results. Despite not revving as high, the L model produced around 88 hp to the rear wheel, still well up on the competition and with a massive increase in midrange torque, particularly around 5,000 rpm. Suzuki got what it wanted: more torque with little horsepower loss.

Another note from the looks-can-be-deceptive department: the L model's chassis was thoroughly revised as well. It essentially had a new frame, picking up elements of the GSX-R1100's, including upper frame tubes that were more splayed outward to improve rigidity. Rake and trail were both increased slightly—by 0.7 degree and 1mm, respectively—for improved stability. The swingarm was also based on the 1100's and stretched the wheelbase to 55.7 inches. This constant alteration of the GSX-R's frame geometry serves to illustrate how closely the company listens to the race teams, continuing the hunt for ideal handling as suspension and tire technologies evolve. The truth is, no one perfect set of numbers can be followed as motorcycle technology as a whole improves.

Somewhat confusing for Americans was the suspension situation. Elsewhere, the '90 J model received a male-slider fork, but the U.S. version kept the previous model's conventional fork. The U.S. market did get the first remote-reservoir shock fitted to the GSX-R that year, along with the rest of the world. Slotted front brake rotors replaced drilled units, and a wider, 170mm-wide rear tire was grafted on.

That would all seem like a lot of work for a motorcycle ostensibly near the end of its product cycle, but such was the competition at the time that Suzuki felt the need to keep the pressure hard on development. "We have always felt the need to push chassis development," explains Hisayuki Sugita, now an assistant manager for motorcycle engineering.

But more was to come. For the 1991 model year, Suzuki released the GSX-R750M, which

ABOVE: Suzuki switched to a 17-inch front wheel for quicker, lighter steering response, which would become the de facto standard for sportbikes. Michelin helped the company develop a new breed of radial tire for the bike as well.

OPPOSITE: Herve Moineau and Patrick Igoa campaigned a GSX-R750 in World Endurance competition. Winning endurance races remained a top priority for Suzuki even as it began to focus on 500 GP, AMA Superbike, and World Superbike series.

carried a new fairing and still more revisions to the engine. The fairing was a relatively easy change. "Aerodynamics was starting to become ever more important," says Mr. Kawaguchi, body designer of the '89 double-R model and the bodywork for the '91 to '95 bikes. "We wanted to keep the GSX-R image in the twin headlights, but a plastic cover was used to make the fairing more streamlined."

The chassis carried over largely intact from the '90 model, but the M's engine got a surprise makeover. Rumors were flying in race paddocks and magazines of Suzuki's imminent switch to liquid cooling. All of its major competition had joined the antifreeze league, and the race teams had to take ever more extreme measures to keep the oil-cooled engine happy in race trim. Oil coolers the size of coolant radiators sprang up. Additional tweaks inside the engine to carefully control oil flow were the norm, yet the engines were still running hotter than desired. By the end of the 1980s, it was clear that Mr. Yokouchi's great idea—so important to the success of the first GSX-R—was nearing the end of its useful life in high-performance and racing machines. Power had come to dominate the proceedings. No surprise to anyone who has met Mr. Yokouchi, in retrospect he is sanguine about the process of changing to liquid cooling: "It was inevitable."

ABOVE: Two significant changes to the GSX-R750 for 1990 are visible here: the remote-reservoir shock, new for the model, and the return to a four-into-one exhaust system with a chamfer at the leading edge of the muffler for increased cornering clearance.

But the world would have to wait a year for Suzuki to finally make the leap. In the interim, the last gasp for the oil-cooled generation received substantial valvetrain updates. All GSX-Rs up to this point used a form of valve actuation that was just about the industry standard. For each pair of valves in the engine—the intakes and exhausts, separately—one cam lobe pressed down on a forked rocker arm. At the free end was a pair of threaded adjusters, which in turn pushed on the valve stems.

This offset system allowed the included valve angle to be smaller than would otherwise be possible if the cams were directly atop the valves. And compared to the direct-acting valve systems of the period, the forked-rocker setup provided less sliding friction. It was useful for the air-cooled, and even the oil-cooled, engines to have some open space atop the combustion chamber for finning or for the oil chamber, so the penalty of having the cams reside ahead of and behind the valve-stem axis wasn't large. Also, by placing the cams off-axis with the valves, the head could be slightly shallower, a useful trait in a time when most engines were comparatively long stroke and fitted into frames whose main members wrapped up over the head. Later, as designers sought to make the

ABOVE LEFT: Suzuki dramatically upgraded the GSX-R's suspension with a remote-reservoir shock featuring adjustable compression and rebound damping. The remote reservoir increased the volume of damping oil and helped the shock run cooler, for more consistent damping under racing conditions. **BELOW LEFT:** Slotted brake rotors and four-piston calipers came straight off the '89 RR model and delivered higher performance under all weather conditions, on and off the racetrack. **BELOW:** This image summed up the competition's view of the GSX-R from the saddle. This was not wishful thinking from Suzuki: at the time the GSX-R continued to set records in the showroom.

TOP: The 1990 GSX-R750 engine returned to its long-stroke roots but, thanks to material improvements, kept the high redline of the short-stroke engine. A new curved oil cooler increased surface area without getting in the way of the hollow-spoke, 17-inch front wheel. **ABOVE LEFT:** "Slingshot" carburetors were retained for the '90 model. They fed a reworked cylinder head that featured slightly smaller valves than the '89 version to promote better midrange power. **ABOVE RIGHT:** A newly developed large-volume single muffler replaced the twin units from the '89 bike, which helped to reduce weight and increase cornering clearance while meeting tougher international noise regulations.

PASS
TIRE APPLICABLE

OPPOSITE: The curved oil cooler made room for the beefier upper tubes of the new inverted fork. The frame, thoroughly revised, still used a cast-aluminum head section.

cylinder head shorter from back to front—mainly to make room for a new breed of downdraft intake systems—the compromises started to come out in favor of direct valve actuation, which remains the standard today.

Elevated engine speeds had exposed the weight of the system and its intolerance of ultra-high revs. With this in mind, Suzuki operated each valve through an individual cam lobe and thin finger follower. At the same time, shims for adjusting valve clearances replaced the screw/locknut setup to help reduce valvetrain weight. Otherwise, the '91 GSX-R750 wasn't much different from the '90, except for the American market, which finally received the Showa inverted fork that the rest of the world had enjoyed a year earlier.

Suzuki's emphasis had always been on the 750, but the 1100 received useful updates through this period and was carefully nurtured into its own niche. The 1100 was intended to be slightly less purposeful and more comfortable because it was not raced, and Suzuki felt that it would be bought by "more mature" riders who could afford the higher price and increased insurance costs. But a careful balance was attempted so that an essential GSX-R-ness would be retained.

A company the size of Suzuki has to use its engineering talent carefully, so although this generation of GSX-R750 started in 1988, the 1100 would soldier on unchanged until 1989. At that point, the 1100 took a shift of sorts, pairing the Katana 1100 engine introduced a year earlier with the frame of the just-revised 750. Created as an 1127cc unit, the Katana engine was a half-generation ahead of the 1052cc engine used in the first-generation 1100s. Nonetheless, it received substantial revisions for use in the new GSX-R1100, including beefed-up bottom-end components and different primary-

LEFT: The '91 GSX-R was beginning to take on a shape it would carry into the liquid-cooled age, but you can tell this is a second-gen bike by the generous side air exits on the fairing. The oil-cooled engine needed every bit of airflow it could get.

RIGHT: Suzuki took the opportunity to revise the instrument panel on the 1991 model. Gone was the foam-encased gauge set, replaced with a more modern iteration. Now the tach started at zero. This panel is fitted on the 1100, identifiable by the clip-ons located above the triple clamp, just visible in the bottom corners of this photo.

BELOW: Suzuki was understandably proud of the GSX-R street bike's kinship to the race bike. Here it is posed with the World Endurance bike. Notice the frame protectors below the tank—they would arrive the following year with the liquid-cooled model.

drive gearing; together with reworked final-drive gearing, the GSX-R1100 emerged taller-geared than the Katana.

The chassis used many of the same components as the 750's but was strengthened, particularly in the cast steering-head area. A 1.3-inch-longer swingarm increased the wheelbase to 56.7 inches. Other differences from the 750 included taller handlebars that were mounted above the upper triple clamp and rubber-covered footpegs. (The 1100 engine wasn't as smooth as the 750.)

As the decade opened, Suzuki knew it would have to recast the GSX-R into a more modern role. The 750 maintained its leg lock on the dyno—no other truly mass-produced 750 of the period could touch it—but the competition was looming in the rearview. The company's decisions for the next generation of GSX-R would prove to be the most challenging in the model's history.

BELOW: This left-side view emphasizes the return to a four-into-one exhaust system for the GSX-R. The frame was again revised with evolutionary changes for increased stiffness.

CHAPTER 4

FACING THE INEVITABLE: LIQUID COOLING

Generation 3: 1992–1995

OPPOSITE: The curved radiator used to chill the new engine wasn't much larger than the oil cooler it replaced, but it was considerably more effective. The liquid-cooled engine had more consistent power output. Its performance was less affected by high ambient temperatures than the oil-cooled model.

BELOW: The GSX-R never wandered far from the track. Much of the bike's development took place on the closed course, and naturally, the move to liquid cooling was a step to ensure future competitiveness. Increased power demands had outstripped the original oil-cooling technology's reach.

Suzuki's management and engineers stood at a crossroads with the GSX-R in the early 1990s. After seven years of racing success—well-deserved wins in AMA Superbike and World Endurance—and strong street bike sales, the direction for the next-generation GSX-R was hotly debated. One thing not up for debate was the switch to a liquid-cooled engine. The engineering team anticipated the inexorable march of horsepower—from the original goal of 100PS (approximately 100 horsepower) up to 110, 120, or even 130 possible from a 750 in the none-too-distant future. Development continued at a vigorous pace, with new computer technologies meshing with the engineer's better understanding of how the GSX-R engine responded to tuning changes. It was an all-out effort to find more power, that's true, but the desire was also to find additional midrange power and, where possible, improve durability without sacrificing performance.

These goals were a big jump from the original GSX-R's horsepower mandate, around which the first oil-cooling scheme was designed. New thinking in combustion chamber shapes and manufacturing technologies that allowed for more precision at lower cost were working along with racing experience to push horsepower up and up.

There were two possible avenues to follow. One: join the majority of the manufacturers who were producing sportbikes in what is, today, a familiar idiom—a narrow inline-four-cylinder engine stuffed into a beam frame whose main members curved around the outside of the cylinder head. This form was used by all of the GSX-R major competitors and, indeed, by Suzuki's own race team on the RG500 GP bike. This direction in frame design would signal a major shift for the appearance and technology of the GSX-R.

Option two was to continue to develop the GSX-R with an over-the-

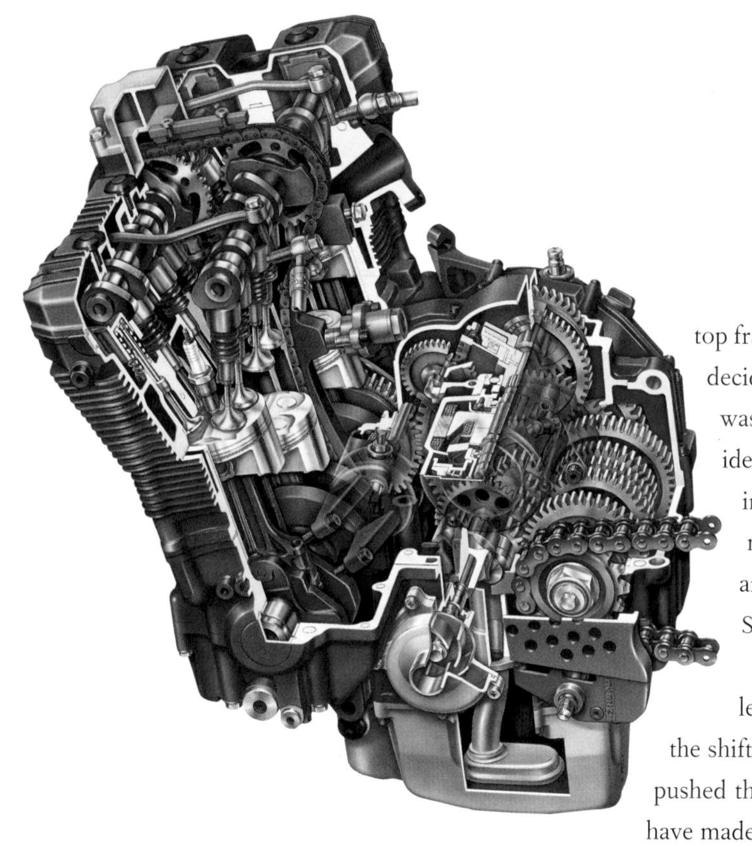

top frame and finally acquiesce to liquid cooling. "It was decided to stay with main elements of the GSX-R. It was believed that that was what riders wanted, that the identity of the GSX-R was wrapped up in the styling and frame design," says Masami Haga, general manager of the motorcycle planning department and a man deeply involved in a lot of the directions Suzuki takes.

The product planners' desire to retain GSX-R legacy appearances was in part a way to help smooth the shift away from the bike's signature oil cooling. But it pushed the engineers into design decisions they would not have made given a clean sheet of paper. For a company that traditionally had let engineers choose the directions they thought best—to, in essence, dictate what the product would be based on the need to have the lightest, fastest, most potent motorcycle in the class—these were tough times. Still, the engineers' solutions were often inspired, despite the bike's general move away from what are considered to be the GSX-R's major tenets: lightness, simplicity, compactness. Power is fine if you have it, but Mr. Yokouchi was clearly right that you could do more with less if the overall motorcycle was very light.

ABOVE: It was the push for more horsepower that drove the engineers to liquid cooling. With that decision made, they could reduce the size of the cylinder block and head and incorporate the direct-action valvetrain they had wanted to use two years before—and still retain a fair portion of the previous engine's bottom end.

OPPOSITE: Once again, Suzuki turned to the racetrack for development. The real impetus for liquid cooling came from the track, as well, even though the engineers had foreseen the day when oil cooling alone wasn't going to be competitive for the street bike.

Times were changing rapidly by the early 1990s, with massive improvements in tires, suspension, and brakes. Speeds were climbing—not just at the racetrack but also for everyday riders on the street—thereby putting greater strain on the chassis. Engine power was always expected to increase, and it flat-out had to in order to keep up with the inevitable weight gain of improved suspension and larger wheels and tires.

For 1992, then, Suzuki unleashed the GSX-R750WN in most markets except the U.S. (Sales of the old bike were still strong in the States, and a slightly weak economy meant that it would be hard to press any price increases on the new model.) America would keep the oil-cooled GSX-R another year with minimal changes and receive the GSX-R750W in 1993.

Practically everything about the liquid-cooled GSX-R was new. The chassis had begun to morph from the original extruded-tube alloy design to something on the way to a true spar design. The extruded upper tubes were now five sided, with a noticeable chamfer along the upper edge. Still, the frame was considered a double-cradle design, with the main tubes arching up and over the engine and making clearance for the cheeks of the airbox on the noisy side of four 38mm Mikuni carburetors.

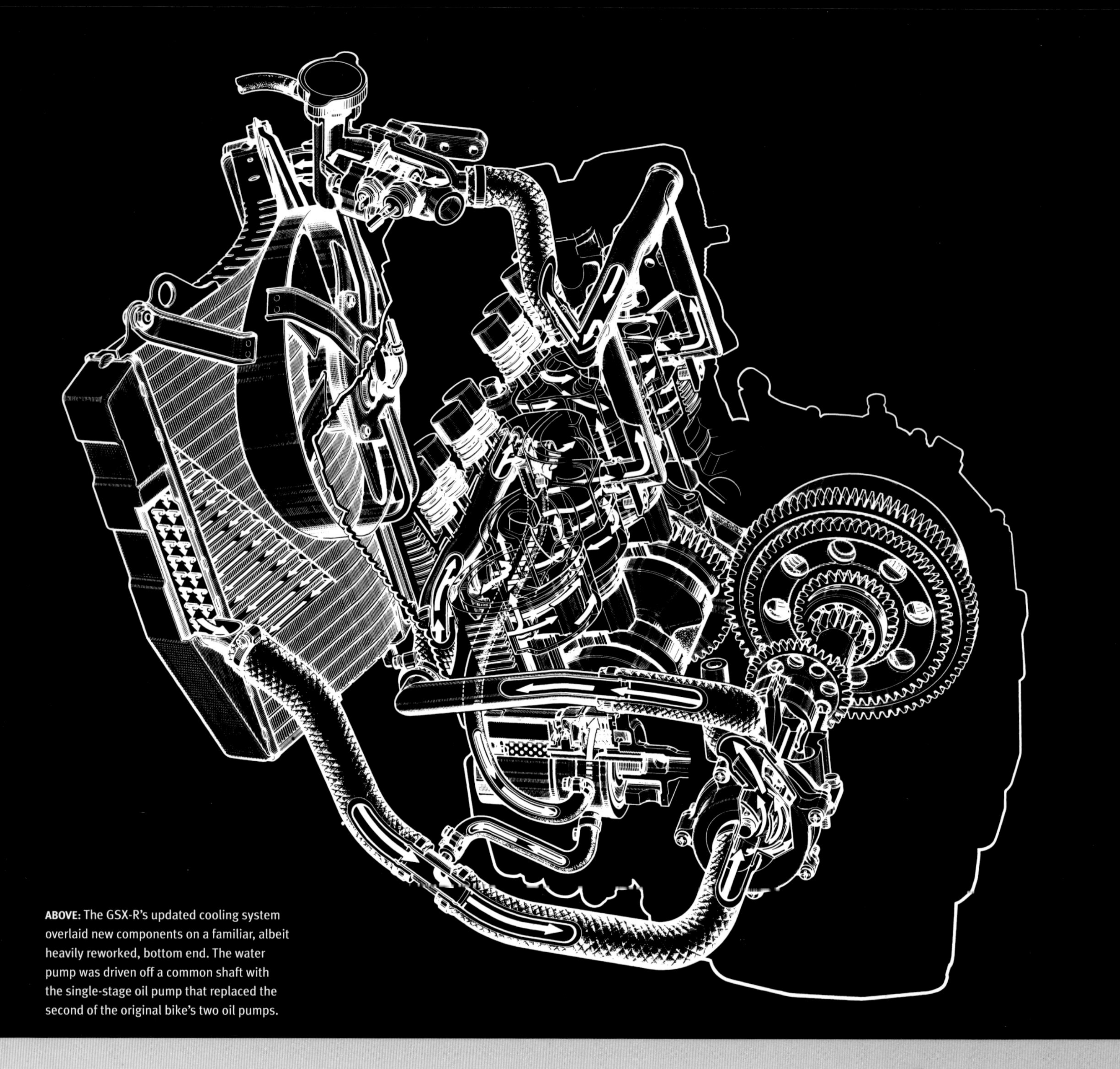

ABOVE: The GSX-R's updated cooling system overlaid new components on a familiar, albeit heavily reworked, bottom end. The water pump was driven off a common shaft with the single-stage oil pump that replaced the second of the original bike's two oil pumps.

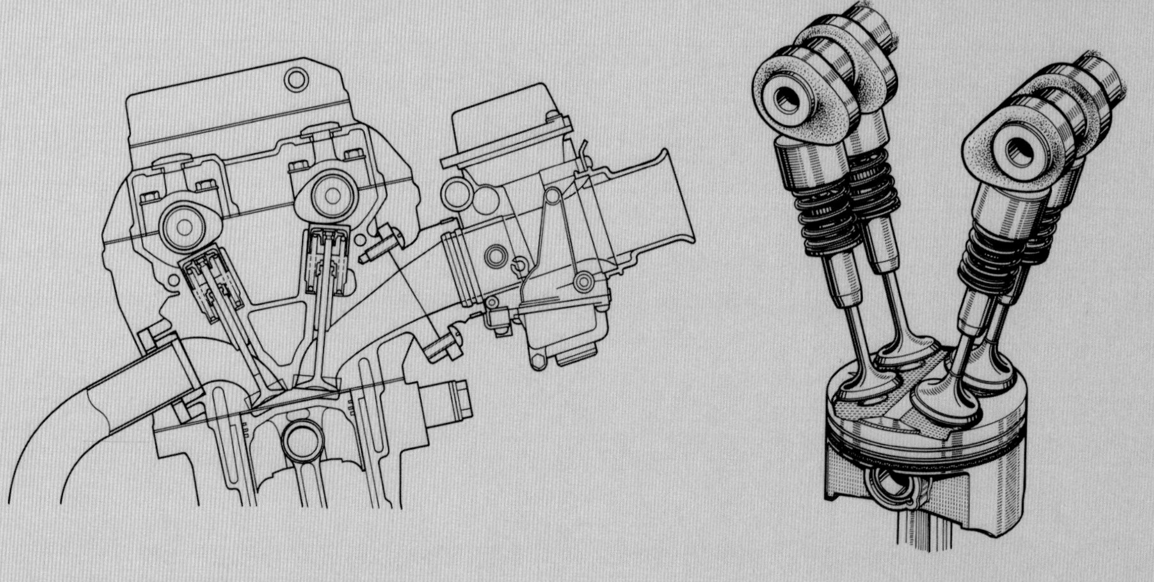

RIGHT: The new, more compact head—especially in its front-to-back dimensions—allowed the intake ports to straighten for improved efficiency. A redesign to the combustion chambers made them flatter than before and capable of handling a higher compression ratio.

FAR RIGHT: With the adoption of direct-action valve gear, Suzuki joined the technological mainstream in the early 1990s. Before then, the cam lobes had acted on either forked or single rockers whose free ends pressed on the valve stems. This new system, a version of which is still in use today, lets the cam lobes actuate the buckets or followers directly. Underneath each lobe, between the bucket and the valve stem, is a small steel adjusting shim. This change permitted a higher redline and increased the valve-adjustment intervals.

Suzuki took the opportunity to push the GSX-R750 along the path that defines sportbike chassis geometry. From the early bikes' "lazy" steering geometry and, for the most part, long wheelbases, the GSX-R first was made shorter and then gradually received ever more aggressive steering-head geometry. For the '92 GSX-R750WN model, rake was reduced yet again (from 25.3 degrees to 24.5), as was trail (3.9 inches down to 3.7). Sportbike steering heads were getting steeper, but wheelbases were growing again; the GSX-R750's increased 0.8 inch to 55.7. As the engineers continued to develop the GSX-R, they found (as did engineers at other factories) that the steeper head helped reduce steering effort and improve maneuverability, and the longer wheelbase helped add back some stability. In place of the previous-generation bike's extruded, square-section swingarm came a fabricated affair of aluminum stampings and castings.

Feedback from racing also shaped the bike's rear subframe, which, for the first time, was a bolt-on affair. This method, as opposed to the welded-on subframe of the previous generation, made for easier modification for the race bikes and simplified repair procedures for both racers and street riders. It was less likely that a mild get-off would bend the main frame or break off the subframe in such a way that the entire frame would have to be replaced.

This bike was recognizable as a GSX-R, even if you didn't immediately figure out the reason for the curious wedge of bodywork covering the rearmost part of the main frame. It was put there "because riders complained about coming in contact with the frame and scratching it," says designer Takahiko Kawaguchi. The upper fairing was largely a carryover from the '91 model except for repositioned air intakes, but the lower fairing clearly revealed the massive new water radiator in front of the engine and the large air exhausts along the flank.

The engine requiring all this new plumbing was essentially new, even though it used the old GSX-R750's 70.0mm by 48.7mm bore and stroke. A completely redesigned cylinder head carried valves the same size as the previous engine's but with thinner stems and set at an included angle of 32 degrees. That's a reduction of 8 degrees from the oil-cooled motor but hardly cutting-edge. In fact, by '94, the GSX-R750 engine seemed to embrace conservative values all around.

BELOW: With liquid cooling providing more even heat dissipation, the engineers had the opportunity to reduce the cylinder bore centers for what became an overall more compact engine. On the previous engine, the gap between the cylinder barrels was a necessary adjunct to the oil cooling. With better heat control, each moving component could be made lighter, which in turn helped reduce the overall size and weight of the engine. Yes, it had an additional system, but the engine was smaller and more easily packaged—moved forward and down—in the chassis.

The valves were actuated directly by the cam lobes, no more rocker arms or finger followers. "Actually, we were ready to make this change in the previous engine," says Kunio Arase, now part of the racing group in charge of the MotoGP and Superbike engines. "But we had a production hang-up. The factory could not produce a direct-acting system before 1992."

Along with the shallower included valve angle for a more efficient combustion chamber came higher compression, now 11.8:1 compared to the 10.9:1 of the last oil-cooled engine. Suzuki could get a lot more heat out of the engine with liquid swirling around the head and upper cylinders, so it could raise the compression ratio without fear of detonation or heat saturation. Curiously, the GSX-R retained vestigial cylinder finning. "The engine didn't need it, of course," says Mr. Arase. "But it was felt that the fins were needed to preserve the family resemblance." In other words, no "naked" engine could be a GSX-R's prime mover. Mr. Arase's comment tells you a lot about his engineering mind. Although he's clearly loath to say so directly, you sense his dissatisfaction with the compromise. Unnecessary finning adds weight and casting complexity, not performance.

Substituting water jackets for full finning allowed Suzuki's engineers to close up the bore spacing, which narrowed the engine by nearly 3 inches. The combination of a more compact head and a thinner bottom end allowed the chassis guys to move the engine forward and down in the frame—almost always a good thing for handling. Suzuki had yet to reach for end-driven cams, preferring to retain the central cam tunnel. (Yamaha did the same during this period, so end drive was hardly expected from anybody.) Suzuki did not abandon oil cooling altogether. The piston squirts remained, and just to make sure the oil remained cool, an oil-to-water cooler was placed at the base of the oil filter.

Because Suzuki stayed with an over-the-top, double-cradle frame, the engine did not have the fashionable downdraft carburetion. Instead, the quartet of Mikunis sat upright, just as the carbs had since the days of the GS750. Although revised for the new GSX-R750WN model, the airbox could not take up as much space as one designed to feed downdraft carburetors.

Ultimately, the new liquid-cooled GSX-R750's engine punched out nearly the same peak power as the previous engine but with a commendably broader torque curve, one that started its hike up the mountain at lower revs. Even when reverted to the long-stroke configuration, the oil-cooled engine made its best power above 9,000 rpm. The new engine was described in contemporary press as coming alive by 7,500 rpm, even if it still packed the most fun from 10,000 rpm to the 13,500 rpm redline.

Continuous improvement in suspension and brake design helped push up the gizmo quotient in every sportbike of the period, and the inevitable result of the GSX-R gaining both a stiffer frame and a liquid-cooled engine was weight gain. The GSX-R750WN was some 60 pounds heavier than the original GSX-R. The bike fought back with much improved handling and better power—

LEFT: The fuel-tank vent, exposed on the first generation of GSX-Rs, was retained for '92. It was not only a nod to the bike's racing heritage but a useful and compact way to make this necessary device work. **BELOW:** The distinctive frame covers on the GSX-R750 were a response to rider complaints that their riding gear could become caught up in and scratch the beautiful, unpainted aluminum frame.

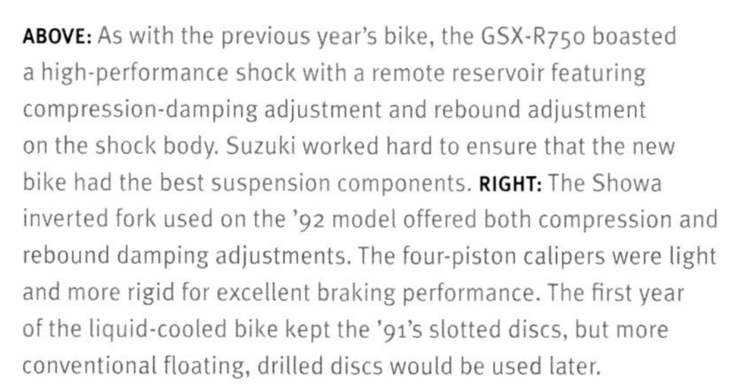

ABOVE: As with the previous year's bike, the GSX-R750 boasted a high-performance shock with a remote reservoir featuring compression-damping adjustment and rebound adjustment on the shock body. Suzuki worked hard to ensure that the new bike had the best suspension components. **RIGHT:** The Showa inverted fork used on the '92 model offered both compression and rebound damping adjustments. The four-piston calipers were light and more rigid for excellent braking performance. The first year of the liquid-cooled bike kept the '91's slotted discs, but more conventional floating, drilled discs would be used later.

OPPOSITE: Aerodynamics played a key role in the GSX-R's development. Suzuki's engineers spent a lot of time in the wind tunnel trying to minimize drag and improve the quality of airflow through and around the bike.

BELOW: Mr. Kawaguchi's draft of the GSX-R styling design isn't much different from the final version. The emphasis for this generation of GSX-R was, as ever, on the mechanicals. But updated styling was a key factor in making the GSX-R remain fresh in an ever-changing sportbiking world.

particularly for the race teams able to harness the benefits of liquid cooling—but the media continued to point out that the GSX-R had drifted away from the original's focus on low weight and utter simplicity. The GSX-R750 had matured—and no one doubts that it had to—but enthusiasts wondered just where Suzuki had put its priorities.

Suzuki, once again, worked fast to counter the complaints. The '94 GSX-R750 received a host of improvements, most of them aiming to reduce overall weight. Using a revised frame, with the wall thicknesses reduced in strategic locations to prevent a loss of rigidity, and costly magnesium covers on the engine along with hollow transmission shafts, Suzuki was able to pull some 30 pounds off the GSX-R750's hide. That's an impressive number, and along with slightly increased power from detail improvements inside the engine, it helped redress the performance gap with the burgeoning 900cc class. For '95, the GSX-R750 was left pretty much alone. Suzuki did not at the time drop the hint—though it did little to stem rumors—but big things were in the works for '96.

Arai
alpinestars

One for All, Big and Small

Suzuki is among the smartest players in the parts-commonality scheme, wherein a manufacturer leverages one set of chassis designs, bodywork, engine cases, and running gear for multiple models, but it set new standards in 1992 with the introduction of the GSX-R600 and, a year later, with the revised GSX-R1100.

The benefits of parts sharing are compelling, especially for Suzuki, which is well versed in stretching its engineering resources to the fullest. Suzuki was a fraction the size of Honda and Yamaha, yet it still managed to maintain a stranglehold on the ultra-sport class. In 1992, U.S. sales of the GSX-R750 were better than 4,000 units. In that same year, Honda sold just fewer than 1,100 750 class machines (the VFR750), and Kawasaki pushed out 2,225 ZX-7s and ZX-7Rs. From this vantage point, it's easy to see how sharing parts among three models—the new 600, introduced to the world in 1992; the 750; and an updated 1100, debuting in 1993—would improve profitability and, if done properly, not endanger the sales of any category.

The 600 was a controversial program. Without the resources to develop a 600 class machine from scratch, the decision was made to adapt the 750 chassis and new liquid-cooled engine to the task. As a result, the 600 shared the 750's frame (with minor modifications) as well as the larger bike's bodywork, wheels, brakes, and basic suspension.

In the early 1990s, the traditional displacement classes were starting to morph. Most manufacturers fielded middleweight machines—500s first, then 550s, and then 600s—as well as 750s and open-class bikes at and above 1000cc. But the market was beginning to stratify in the early 1990s, with ever more powerful and sophisticated 600s taking sales from the 750s left and right. Partly, this phenomenon stemmed from the rising cost of street bikes and ever-increasing insurance requirements. Suddenly, a 600 class machine looked considerably cheaper to buy and own than a 750, while the liter bikes were still an atmosphere away. By 1993, the GSX-R750's only competition was the Kawasaki ZX-7. The Honda VFR750 had changed into a sport-tourer with the arrival of the lighter, very fast CBR900RR. Yamaha's FZR750 had been gone from the U.S. market since the end of 1988. (Its replacement, the YZF750R, would return for 1994, miss 1995, and be gone again by 1998.)

The market was quickly changing, with 600s a required component of any sportbike line, 900s taking over for 750s (the theory was to have more power in a 750-size package), and the big bikes turning into quasi GTs with thrilling top-speed performance.

OPPOSITE: Take a closer look at the redesigned fairing. Note that the side exits have fewer holes—liquid cooling made airflow needs simpler.

BELOW: Suzuki produced a limited quantity of GSX-R750 SPs for the European market. While the bike was mechanically identical to the GSX-Rs offered to America, they played even more heavily on the racetrack prowess of the bike. Notice the use of a blacked-out section of the rearmost side panel made to look like a competition numberplate.

OPPOSITE: For the 1100, Suzuki increased chassis stiffness by using additional engine hangers on both sides of the frame. Such a move was warranted by the greater power of the 1100 engine allied to the added traction from the larger rear tire.

BELOW: The new 750 frame employed the traditional combination of materials technology—cast, extruded, and stamped aluminum—in a format familiar to every GSX-R enthusiast. Through a comprehensive reinforcement and strengthening program, the frame was also more rigid than before.

When Suzuki tackled the 600 class in the U.S. by basing its machine off the 750, the resulting bike was larger and heavier than the other 600s, albeit with higher-specification brakes and suspension. (Now that all the top-line 600s wear inverted forks, it's easy to forget that Suzuki was there first.) Adding to the perception of heft, the 600 had slightly more conservative chassis numbers, with 1 degree more rake, 0.2 inch more trail, and 0.2 inch more wheelbase.

For the engine, Suzuki's engineers specified smaller, 65.0mm pistons (down from the 750's 70.0mm units) and a short-stroke crank, giving a total stroke of 45.2mm, 3.5mm less than the 750. They didn't have enough development time to extract the most from this configuration, so the 600 arrived larger than its competition and slightly down on power. It should be no surprise that the proud parents were loath to watch their offspring take such a drubbing, and Suzuki stopped production of the 600 after the '93 model year.

The revised GSX-R1100 fared much better. As before, it lagged one year behind the big changes brought to the 750. The '93 received the liquid-cooled configuration from an engine that shared a great many parts with the 750. Acknowledging that the 1100 would be plenty powerful in a 750-size frame, Suzuki's engineers worked on maximizing torque. The new engine's bore and stroke dimensions—75.5mm by 60.0mm—were considerably less oversquare than the 750's or 600's. Both of the smaller engines' bore to stroke ratios were 1.45:1; the 1100's was a considerably more conservative 1.25:1. What's more, by using carburetors the same size as the 750's and comparatively small valves, the 1100 engine made prodigious torque. *Cycle World* described the revised 1100's engine as having "excellent manners": "Around town, the engine is a docile partner, and offers the rider a plentiful supply of smooth, torquey, low-vibration power." The magazine went on to say, "Forceful acceleration begins as low as 4,000 rpm, and builds in a linear fashion to the bike's 11,500 rpm redline.

The 8,500 rpm burst of last year's model is missing."

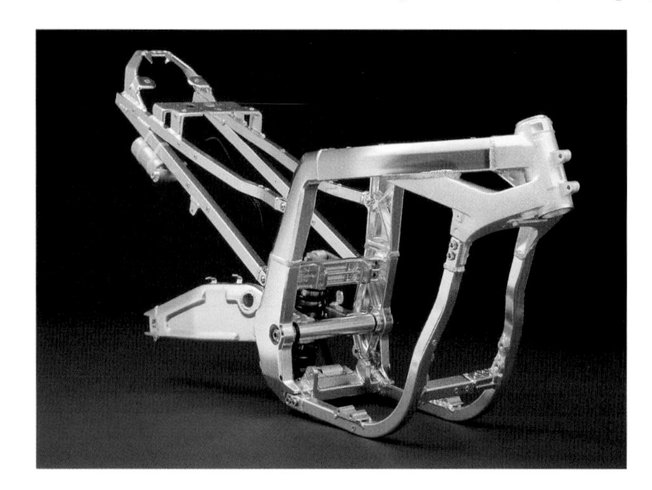

In keeping with the established philosophy that the 1100 wasn't as deadly serious as the 750 and therefore should be slightly more comfortable, the 1100 once again came with clip-on handlebars above the top triple clamp. The new frame pushed back the rider slightly to make room for the larger main members and an enlarged airbox, but the change was largely mitigated by the taller bars.

Suzuki continued to develop the GSX-R line aggressively, of course. But in retrospect, this third generation can be seen as a side trip away from the bike's principal intentions as a

DGM
MADE IN
JAPAN
MIKUNI
CORP.

OPPOSITE: Thomas Stevens is aboard the Yoshimura Superbike at Laguna Seca in 1994. Notice the additional cooling slits in the nose of the fairing—an effort to increase overall cooling of the engine in race trim. Although Suzuki had moved to liquid cooling for this generation, racing demands pushed even that system to the limit.

BELOW: Suzuki continued to use endurance racing as the crucible to prove the design integrity and help drive the development process. This is Alex Barros's GSX-R750 from the Suzuka 8 Hours in 1993.

race-ready Superbike. With this iteration, it had grown large and soft, and the competition's performance crowded it more than ever before. The GSX-R had been a tremendous success for the company, a massive seller, and a gold-clad marketing tool. The product-planning and marketing staffs had the advantage in product development, and they were rightly concerned that a move too far away from what a GSX-R looked like might jeopardize its success. And even in a softening U.S. economy and with amazing new sportbikes stealing some of the GSX-R's thunder, the line continued to sell extremely well for Suzuki. Such reliable income was important to maintain the GSX-R's place in racing as well as to support the Grand Prix team. Kevin Schwantz, now considered legend in Japan, won the top crown for Suzuki in 1993, eleven years after the last 500GP title with Franco Uncini.

But what the marketing types had failed to realize was that Mr. Yokouchi and the engineers—even the engineers working on this generation—were right: performance mattered most. Above and beyond all: performance. A decade on, the engineers responsible for this generation of GSX-R squirm in their chairs slightly, tacitly acknowledging that maintaining GSX-R appearances had trumped maintaining the GSX-R's original performance brief.

All that was about to change.

MOTUL
SUZUKI
MOTUL
SUZUKI

agv
SUZUKI
SUZUKI

CHAPTER 5

A REVOLUTION RENEWED

Generation 4: 1996–1999

OPPOSITE: Suzuki took the opportunity with the fourth generation redesign to create a smaller, more compact motorcycle. One of the benefits was that the ergonomic profile changed considerably, starting the trend toward ever more compact layouts that continues today. At the same time, the riding position was designed to better facilitate the rider's hanging off for optimum weight distribution during cornering.

A decade after the last of the "legacy" GSX-Rs rolled off the line, the engineers who were in place for its gestation are quick to move on to the next chronological topic. They are in no way ashamed of the 1992–95 GSX-Rs—which were, after all, extremely successful for Suzuki on many levels—but what the company had in store for the next generation was nothing short of astonishing. And they're eager to talk about the effort.

In many ways, the 1996 GSX-R750T was as much a departure for Suzuki and as daring a leap into the future of sportbiking as the original GSX-R. It opened up new technological avenues for the company, causing it to rethink a considerable portion of its engineering efforts in addition to pushing its suppliers and production division to embrace new forms and higher expectations. The '96 GSX-R also had finally broken free of the long shadow cast by Mr. Yokouchi's amazing machine: no longer did the GSX-R have to look like the classical notion of a GSX-R. Say so-long to fins on a liquid-cooled engine. Offer a wave of good-bye to the over-the-top alloy frame.

Welcome, instead, a move toward the mainstream of sportbike design that did not copy what Honda, Kawasaki, and Yamaha were doing but dramatically advanced the state of the art. Low weight was back in style. High horsepower had moved up the menu. Function had, once more, pushed form aside and asserted itself.

"The GSX-R750T was a big step forward for us," says Kunio Arase, who spearheaded the engine effort for this generation. "Much of what we did with that engine we wanted to do earlier, but we were held back by production concerns. Our casting technology was not advanced enough to do much of what we wanted with this new engine family." Better late than never, so they say.

Again, context is useful. Honda had dramatically reset the weight/performance expectations with the CBR900RR, a bike sized like a middleweight but packing a near-liter bike

BELOW: The fourth generation GSX-R750, was no less an object of Suzuki's technological prowess and racing acumen than the original 1985 GSX-R. It embodied then-current race technologies in a way that allowed for a competitive racing machine and, seemingly against all odds, a vastly better, more streetable sportbike. More to the point, the bike was lighter than the previous iteration, bringing the brand back around to being the lightest and most powerful in the class.

LEFT: Scott Russell aboard the GSX-R750 at Daytona in 1996 was a strong performer on a new bike that was still being developed on the racetrack. This generation of GSX-R would begin the utter domination of AMA Superbike and Supersport racing just ahead.

RIGHT: Jamie Whitham rode a GSX-R750 in World Superbike in 1997. For Suzuki this was a development year in WSB without fielding a full factory effort. Whitham's eighth place in the season-ending standings made him the top-finishing Suzuki rider that year.

punch. It was certainly popular enough in the U.S. but it was a sales steamroller in Europe, a very strong market at the beginning of the 1990s. Kawasaki continued to develop the ZX-7 and, unbeknownst to Suzuki, was readying an updated model, the ZX-7R, for '96 that featured a significant weight reduction. Kawasaki had also done well with the ZX-9R, offering a relatively comfortable sportbike with performance that beat the '95 GSX-R750 and dramatically less weight than the GSX-R1100. Yamaha's 750 was more expensive than its nearest competitors and failed to sell well in 1994—technically there was no '95 model in the U.S. Yamaha was expected to return for '96.

All around sportbiking, performance was on the rise and weight was on the way down. The trends of the previous few years were playing out. Big-inch bikes continued to get faster and larger, which suited Suzuki as it watched the liter class closely and elected to continue the GSX-R1100 through 1998 with minor changes; it retained the first generation of water-cooled engine, traditional GSX-R double-cradle frame, and bodacious power. The 1100 retained its mantle of asphalt-searing torque and seriousness of intent.

But the 600cc sportbikes had become the hottest class in town, offering a lot of performance for the dollar. The scene was being set for the obsolescence of the 750 class. Theoretically this category was caught in the middle—not as much raw performance as a full-liter bike and without the feathery handling and accommodating powerband of the 600s. No one in the press would blame Suzuki for leaving the 750 class behind.

Except that Suzuki had other plans. The new GSX-R750 would return with a vengeance to the light-is-right mantra, forcing many riders to question the belief that the only way to get a low-mass sportbike was to buy a 600. Consider the numbers: dry weight of 395 pounds, nearly 50 below the

LEFT AND BELOW: On so many levels, the combination of a young Mat Mladin and the ever-improving GSX-R750, campaigned by the Yoshimura team in AMA Superbike, marks the beginning of Suzuki's domination of AMA racing. Shown here in 1998, Mr. Mladin would finish third overall that season and begin to show the form that would take him to an unprecedented five AMA Superbike championships in six years. What's more, much of what Yoshimura would learn in '98 and '99 with the race bike would be shared with factory engineers to be incorporated into the next-generation street bike.

ABOVE: With the new-generation GSX-R, Suzuki extended its grasp further into the near-stock classes. This is a GSX-R600 prepared for 600cc Supersport racing. With continued help from Yoshimura Japan, informed by feedback from the American racing team, the GSX-R would become a serious player in the stock and mildly modified classes. **RIGHT:** Although the GSX-R1100 did not gain any of the new technology used in the revised 750 and 600 models, it remained a powerful, iconic motorcycle that sold well and had a devoted following of big-bore sportbike enthusiasts.

SUZUKI
GSXR
TOKICO

previous liquid-cooled GSX-R750, and 125 crankshaft horsepower. Close, dangerously close, to the 900 class machines.

Suzuki achieved these laudable numbers in a way totally familiar to GSX-R fans, by scrutinizing every component, every shape, every choice of material on the motorcycle. In this quest for low weight, nothing was sacred. Except it had to be an inline-four. When the engineering team today is asked about alternative layouts, they answer almost in unison, "No. The inline-four is the best configuration." Period. End of discussion.

Yet, in the new GSX-R power plant, nothing of the old remains. From the bottom up, Suzuki created a unique three-level crankcase assembly, with two major split lines—one on the crankshaft axis and one just below for the two transmission gears. There is another split where the cylinder assembly fits into the upper third of the main case, another (obviously) at the head, and another at the oil pan. Traditionally, the overall length of the engine is set by the space required to pack the crankshaft, primary drive, clutch, main transmission, and countershaft along a single axis. It's possible to shrink the engine's length by making the transmission smaller, but this tactic can sacrifice strength in the face of ever-increasing engine power. The other possibility is to stagger the gears to place the transmission's mainshaft below the crankshaft, which allows everything else to move forward.

Suzuki placed the crankcase splits at an angle from horizontal, actually perpendicular to the bore axis for increased strength. It's a fine balance. Cant the cylinders way forward and you'll achieve a desirable front-end weight bias at the risk of making the engine effectively longer. Modern inline-engine sportbikes, with their steep steering geometries, have precious little room to spare between the front wheel and the exhaust system.

It was becoming more common for sportbike manufacturers to build engines with the cylinder block cast as one with the top of the crankcase, but Suzuki didn't follow this trend for a simple reason: its engineers anticipated building more than one displacement from one engine design. Design a single monoblock assembly, and you're instantly limited in what you can do with bore and stroke measurements. Bore can expand or contract slightly, depending upon how beefy the cylinder liners are designed to be, but stroke is trickier. Move to a shorter stroke than the original design without changing the deck height, and there will be more cylinder wall than is necessary. In turn, the connecting rods will need to be longer, which may or may not be to the engine's mechanical advantage but surely will not help weight. On the other side, engineers trying to make a 750 into a 1000, for example, face another set of challenges if the relationship between the crank main bearings and cylinder-head surface cannot be easily modified. Suzuki's solution allows for a relatively simple

OPPOSITE: Suzuki maintained its focus on the 750 class with the fourth-generation bike and allocated its resources toward both Superbike racing and the fast-growing 600cc middleweight class. As a result, it was expected that the 1100 could remain in its former configuration—second-generation liquid-cooled engine in an over-the-top alloy frame—and still remain competitive.

ABOVE: The fourth generation GSX-R750's bodywork was entirely new and distinctive. The raised rear cowling was a pure aerodynamic consideration. By permitting the air to rejoin smoothly behind the bike, drag was reduced, but it also made it more difficult for the bike to be drafted on the racetrack.

change of the cylinder casting to accommodate changes in bore and stroke without tearing up the blueprints on the rest of the bottom end.

For the new 750, Suzuki aimed to make the engine as compact as possible. The previous engine was based heavily on the earlier oil-cooled model, so the bore spacing was wider than it really needed to be in a purely water-cooled engine, and the central cam drive was less compact than the end-drive that appeared on the new engine. (An air-cooled engine worked well with a central cam drive because it created a cooling passage between the two hottest cylinders and kept from blanking one of the end cylinders as would an end-drive system. Advancing technology—stronger cases, stiffer cranks, more precise drive systems—helped make end-driven cams compact *and* accurate.)

By moving the cam drive to the end, the cylinder bores could be moved very close together, further reducing engine width. In the 750, Suzuki used a special plating process that applied a nickel-silicon-carbide coating to the aluminum block casting and called it SCEM, for Suzuki composite electro-chemical material. This long-wearing surface doesn't just create a lighter block; it also transmits combustion heat to the water jackets more efficiently than traditional steel liners. The 750 is an open-deck design, with exposed water jackets fully encircling the bores. With the engine now 1.2 inches narrower than the previous 750, Suzuki could abandon the behind-the-cylinders alternator placement with its associated gearing and turn to a compact unit on the left end of the crankshaft. This change simplified the engine and helped lower its overall center of gravity. That tiny increment of power required to turn the alternator gear was put back into the drivetrain.

Those SCEM-lined bores were home to 72mm pistons, a 2mm increase over the '95 GSX-R750

LEFT AND BOTTOM: Revised through and through, the bike's bodywork nevertheless maintained the family relationship in the headlight treatment, using side-by-side beams shielded by a plastic cover. It was important to the styling designers to create a visual link to the previous GSX-Rs and maintain a family heritage, even though the mechanicals of the bike were completely different. **BELOW:** Both the fourth-generation GSX-Rs started out with Mikuni carburetors. (These are from the 600, introduced in 1997.) Emissions regulations were becoming ever more strict, and it took quite a lot of development to make carbureted motorcycles with good drivability characteristics that also met the regulations.

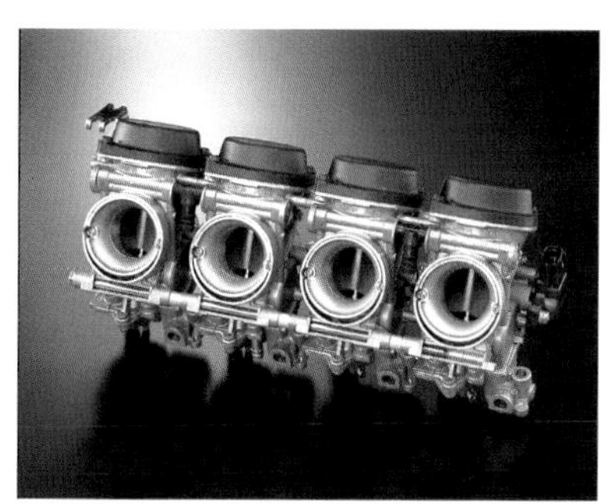

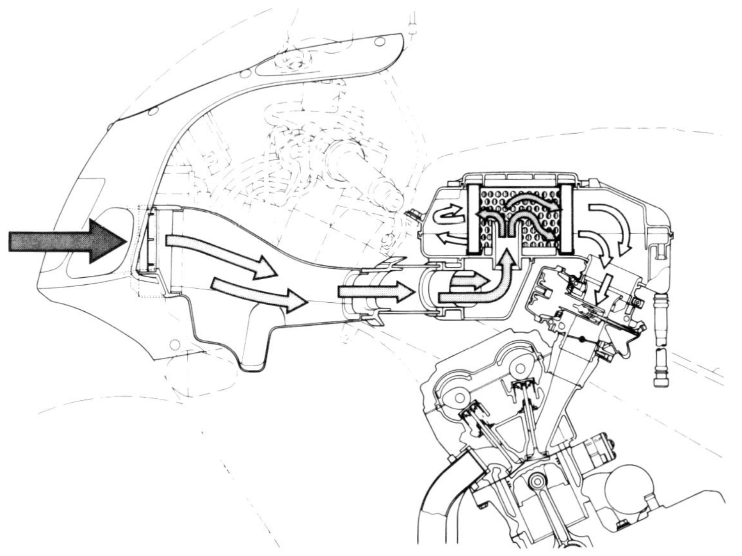

ABOVE: True ram-air ducts arrived with this generation of GSX-R—for both the 600 and the 750. Fairing-mounted apertures gave cool, dense air a direct path to the new, larger airbox. The carburetors' float bowls were linked to the airbox pressure so that as the ram-air effect increased with speed, the overall mixture would remain stable.

but still shy of the very short-stroke '88–'89 bikes. Stroke for the '96 bike was reduced from 48.7mm to 46mm, making way for a 13,500 rpm redline. Oil jets cooled the pistons, just as on the original GSX-R, but now from a gallery in the case itself. No longer did the 750 have an oil cooler in the conventional sense. In place of the familiar radiator, Suzuki used a simple oil-to-water heat exchanger at the base of the oil filter.

Everything changed at the cylinder head, too. The included valve angle was pulled in to 29 degrees, which helped create a more compact and efficient combustion chamber. The compression ratio remained at 11.8:1, but efficiency was clearly up based on comparative dyno charts of the period. Despite packing considerably more top-end power, the new 750 also had more midrange punch than the outgoing GSX-R750.

With this generation, Suzuki joined the industry in using downdraft carburetors, in this case a special set of 39mm Mikunis with electronically controlled slide management. A solenoid controlled by the ignition computer managed an air passage linked to the top of the carburetor slide chamber. Under certain circumstances—low rpm, for example—the system would prevent the slides from rising too quickly, preventing low-speed stumbling that would otherwise occur with such large carburetors. This idea would, of course, return in totally electronic form in the 2000 GSX-R750, which is perhaps as good an indication as any that thoughtful engineers rarely put ideas in the trash but save them for another day. A straight-shot intake tract is more efficient, but there's more to it than that. Kevin Cameron, in the December 1995 *Cycle World*, explained the new system: "Lift the tank, pull the airbox cover, and look down the carbs with a light; you will plainly see the valves. The more streamlined the port, the smaller it can be made for a given airflow. Smaller ports make midrange."

With the four carbs now pointing straight up, the airbox moved from behind the engine—right in the path of hot air—up under the forward edge of the fuel tank, where orthodoxy says it should be even today. This change, in turn, allowed Suzuki to fit real ram-air induction for the first time, via large tubes and reinforced pass-throughs in the main frame out to a pair of ovoid ducts on the face of the fairing.

The new engine's features would not have worked in the old frame, of course, but they didn't have to. Suzuki had been campaigning its RG500 Gamma race bike in international 500GP, and its star rider, Kevin Schwantz, was on the way to the World Championship for 1993 when the '96 GSX-R was being developed. With the mandate to return to race bike technology—spurred on by Schwantz's success—the engineering team chose to emulate the RG500 Gamma as much as possible.

This desire, as much as the drive to reduce weight and improve handling, pushed the engineers to a twin-spar frame. Suddenly, the bike could be smaller and lighter. Wheelbase shrank by 1.5 inches

OPPOSITE: Suzuki's new engine was a dramatic departure from the '95 model's, which had been based on the original GSX-R's power plant. Suzuki also introduced an engine architecture that set the main crankcase parting lines at an angle, with the transmission shafts and the crankshaft separated by an intermediate case. This technique let the transmission be snug up against the crankshaft without the side effect of reducing the gear size.

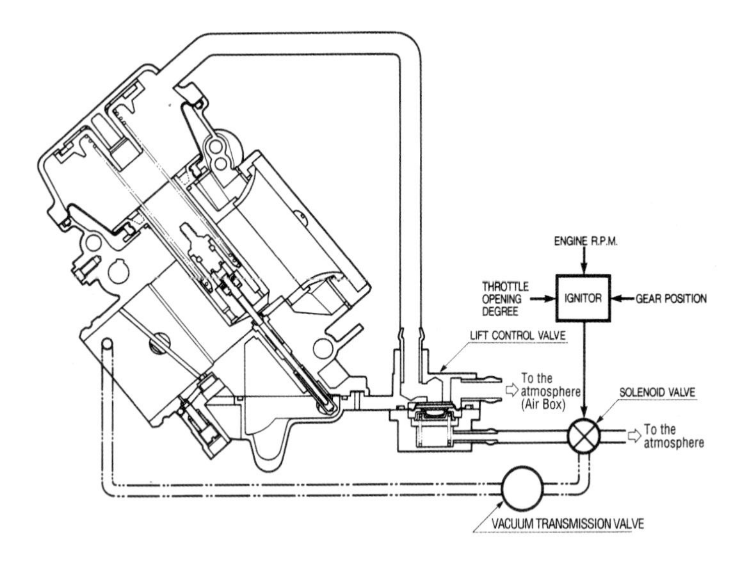

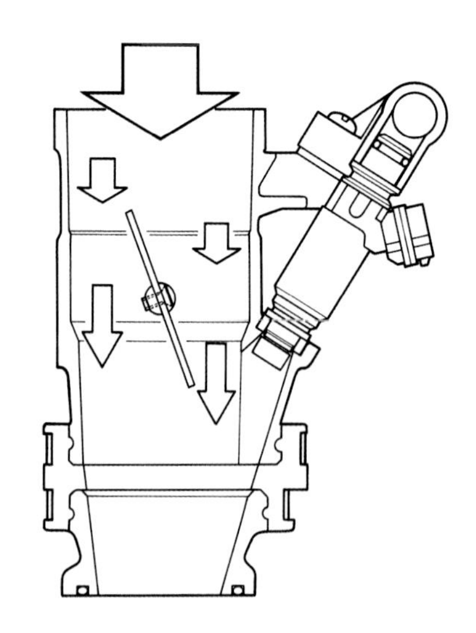

LEFT: Suzuki wanted the GSX-R750 to have class-leading power, and that meant allowing the engine to breathe deeply. However, large carburetors are often difficult to tune for low-speed, snap-open throttle response. Suzuki and Mikuni's answer was a slide-lift system that helped keep the slides under more positive control during low-rpm acceleration. When instructed by the engine control unit, a small valve opened to control the relative pressure in the vacuum diaphragm above the throttle slides. This technology permitted Suzuki to tune the engine for maximum high-rpm power while retaining excellent drivability.

RIGHT: For 1998, Suzuki replaced the GSX-R750's four 39mm carburetors with an electronic fuel injection system with large, 46mm throttle bodies. The Mikuni fuel injectors were controlled by a Denso computer. The performance boost was some 5 hp at the top and, just as important, a smoother torque curve and improved drivability.

to 55—shorter, even, than the stubby CBR900RR. Rake came in by 0.5 degree to 24, even while trail increased slightly to 3.8 inches. The frame itself was made up of familiar materials—castings at the steering head and swingarm pivot—with new vertical extensions to meet the alloy subframe along with a few extruded pieces and stamped-and-welded main spar pieces. The massively braced swingarm was also made up of stamped and extruded aluminum pieces, with some cast items thrown in for good measure. Suzuki had learned to be resourceful in design to use materials in ways that would minimize cost, hence the variety.

Typically, the running gear was updated considerably. Six-piston front brake calipers replaced the four-pot items from '95. The rear wheel was now up to 6 inches wide and wore a massive 190/50-17 tire, up from the 170/60 on the '95 bike.

Suzuki wrapped the new technology in sleek bodywork styled by Toshiyuki Nishino. "Engineering dictated the placement of all the major components, of course," he says. "One of the big challenges was to create a pleasing shape to the fuel tank while still having some capacity. The airbox was quite large." The tank also had to follow the frame with a minimum of visual fuss, which made it quite deep near the back. "We used contrasting paint across that corner of the tank to reduce its visual depth," recalls Mr. Nishino.

That tail hump? Strictly for racing. "We did wind-tunnel tests," explains Mr. Nishino, "and found that this shape was more efficient and made the airflow behind the bike smoother." In other words, the hump made it harder for following racers to draft.

Contemporary press reports praised the new GSX-R lavishly: "The results of our performance testing were truly eye opening," said *Cycle World* of its March 1996 road test. "The GSX-R blazed through the Carlsbad Raceway quarter-mile in 10.61 seconds at an astounding 132.68 mph. Then, during high-speed testing at our top-secret, high-desert test site, it uncorked a mind-blowing 167.5 mph pass. This was balanced against a 165.3 mph run in the other direction, however, yielding a 166 mph average.... These figures are absolutely unreal for a 750, and are more in line with open-class machines." Two months later, *Cycle World* named it the "Ultimate Sportbike" against such luminaries as the Ducati 916 and Honda CBR900RR.

BELOW: This early mock-up of the instrument cluster is very much like the final product. Styles were changing, and the dramatically asymmetrical tach/speedo arrangement was still in the GSX-R's future. The white-faced tach helped distinguish it from the speedo, an effective design.

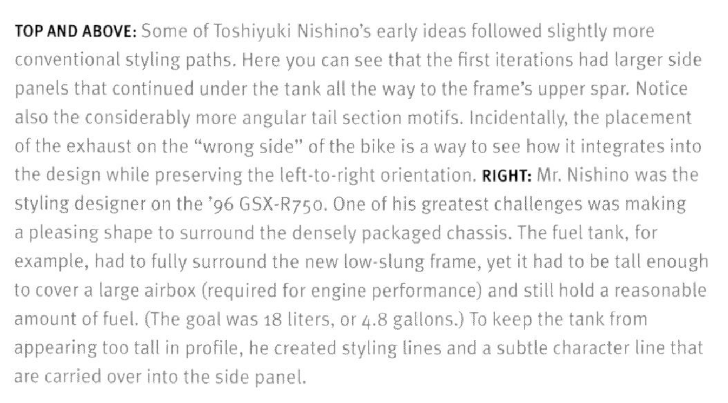

TOP AND ABOVE: Some of Toshiyuki Nishino's early ideas followed slightly more conventional styling paths. Here you can see that the first iterations had larger side panels that continued under the tank all the way to the frame's upper spar. Notice also the considerably more angular tail section motifs. Incidentally, the placement of the exhaust on the "wrong side" of the bike is a way to see how it integrates into the design while preserving the left-to-right orientation. **RIGHT:** Mr. Nishino was the styling designer on the '96 GSX-R750. One of his greatest challenges was making a pleasing shape to surround the densely packaged chassis. The fuel tank, for example, had to fully surround the new low-slung frame, yet it had to be tall enough to cover a large airbox (required for engine performance) and still hold a reasonable amount of fuel. (The goal was 18 liters, or 4.8 gallons.) To keep the tank from appearing too tall in profile, he created styling lines and a subtle character line that are carried over into the side panel.

BELOW: Suzuki developed a paint scheme for the fourth-generation GSX-R featuring a prominent slash of color carried through the fairing and onto the side of the fuel tank. Again, a carefully placed bit of graphic design can change the apparent size of the components.

Kent Kunitsugu, editor of *Sport Rider*, recalls: "The '96 model GSX-R750 was the groundbreaker for Suzuki. It not only shattered the previous performance standards for the class, it also created a benchmark for the sportbike world, regardless of displacement. One needed only to look at the grids of both professional and amateur races swollen with GSX-Rs that year (and for many years afterward) to realize that Suzuki had indeed created the winner—both in the dealerships and on the racetracks—they were looking for. That GSX-R created a whole new arms race between the manufacturers that has not abated since. And we're all the luckier for it."

Without question, Suzuki had hit its mark. Glowing magazine reviews were followed by brisk sales. The machine that many critics believed had rested upon its laurels for too long was suddenly, vigorously back in the fight.

And it was starting to make a mark in racing. "The '96 bike was a huge improvement for us," says Don Sakakura, racing manager for Yoshimura in the U.S. "Racing is hard on the machines. We had some trouble with the cooling of the ['95 and earlier] bikes. But it was better than the oil-cooled engine. Hot running led to a lot of distortion in the head and barrels. Maybe the radiators weren't as good as they are now. We played with different-size coolers all the time. Suzuki started sending us much bigger coolers; some of them were three rows deep."

The new engine was not only more powerful but far more consistent on the racetrack. And the new chassis was an improvement as well. "The GSX-R became a much more neutral motorcycle. On the track, it didn't do anything bad, or exceptionally well, but it was consistent," says Mr. Sakakura. Consistency in racing is sometimes its own reward.

Yoshimura's boat was raised by more than just the tide of a new motorcycle. In '96, an Australian by the name of Mat Mladin joined Yoshimura. Continues Mr. Sakakura: "Mat is a very intense competitor. From a team's perspective, he has a lot of influence. He's a machine on the motorcycle; he's fast and very repeatable. He could go out and do laps on consistent times and give us incredible feedback: thorough, accurate, repeatable. The development cycle of that period really accelerated when Mat came to the team. The results came much quicker." With those results came a renewed respect from the home office. "Suzuki followed our lead in development," says Mr. Sakakura. "As a result, we were able to compete." At the same time Suzuki was churning away with Yoshimura for an AMA Superbike title, the GSX-R was mopping up in the Superstock class.

And still there were improvements waiting in the wings. "Aspects [of design] we hadn't had to consider in the early days were things like recycling and emissions," says Sadayuki Inobe, managing director of Suzuki. In fact, increasing emissions regulations had begun to force compromises in jetting for certain markets, including the U.S. Carburetors are inexpensive and may have a nice "human" feel

BELOW: This illustration is much closer to final production. The aerodynamic tail hump has been integrated into the design, and the fuel tank, which now completely closes in above the frame, is more fully realized.

when jetted properly, but they're hard to get set up with emissions in mind. To that end, Suzuki fitted the '98 GSX-R750 with a Denso-controlled injection system using Mikuni throttle bodies and injectors. A rack of 46mm throttle bodies replaced the 39mm carburetors and provided a slight (5 hp) increase in peak power but much-improved "carburetion" in the midrange. *Cycle World* said, "We found none of the off-idle surging evident with the previous model's too-lean carburetion."

Suzuki was an early adopter of fuel injection for Supersport motorcycles, a feature that is completely common today. At the time, few performance bikes had anything but conventional carburetors, and riders of the time recall that some of the jetting required to meet emissions left a lot to be desired from a ridability standpoint. Suzuki's system was better, but almost as important, it gave the engineers useful experience developing and tuning such a system for a lightweight motorcycle with a powerful, low-crank-mass engine, one of the most difficult applications there is. This is development experience that would hold Suzuki in extremely good stead in the years to come.

Also in store for the '98 machine—the '97 was essentially unchanged from the '96—were juggled cam specifications, a revised airbox with electronic flapper valve, and subtly altered headers aimed at improving midrange power. Weight-saving measures included a thinner primary gear drive and a smaller chain—a #525 replaced the previous #530.

ABOVE LEFT: Because the 600 and 750 engines shared a lot of parts, Suzuki had to find ways of reducing weight on the 600. With less power than the 750, certain stresses were lower on the 600, so the engineers could lighten some parts. One solution was to use tapered bolts holding the crankcase modules together.

BELOW LEFT: Coil-on-plug ignition debuted with the GSX-R600 and found its way onto the 750 in 1998. This technology makes for a hotter, more reliable spark and reduces weight. Moreover, it makes it easier to configure ignition maps to treat each cylinder independently. Although Suzuki did not employ cylinder stagger—giving each cylinder its own ignition map—with this generation, it would with the upcoming models.

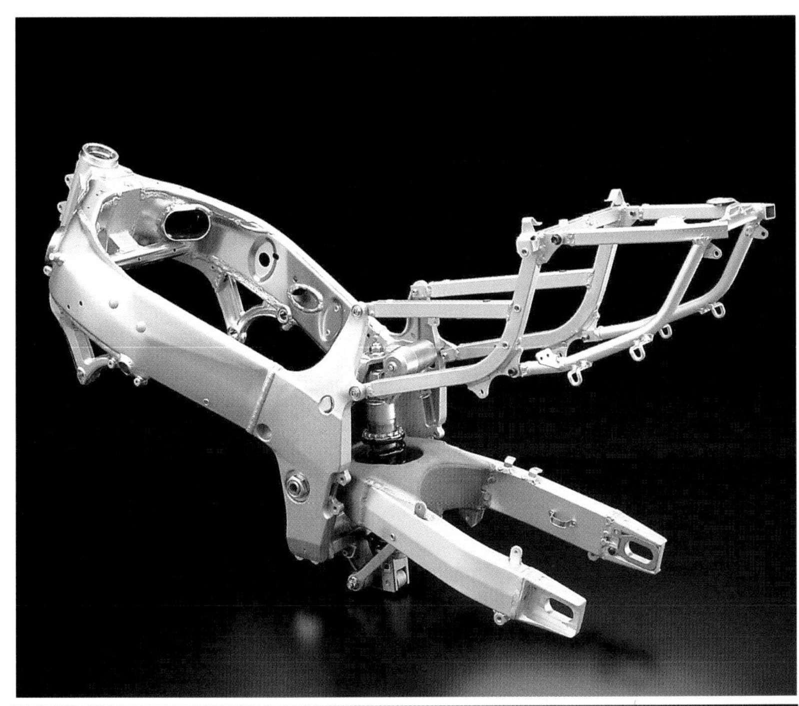

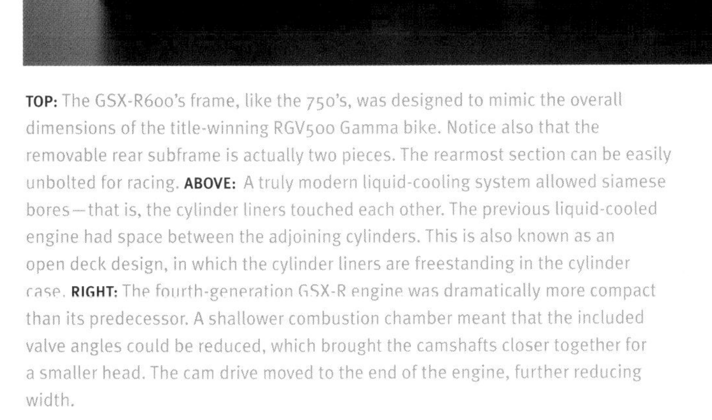

TOP: The GSX-R600's frame, like the 750's, was designed to mimic the overall dimensions of the title-winning RGV500 Gamma bike. Notice also that the removable rear subframe is actually two pieces. The rearmost section can be easily unbolted for racing. **ABOVE:** A truly modern liquid-cooling system allowed siamese bores—that is, the cylinder liners touched each other. The previous liquid-cooled engine had space between the adjoining cylinders. This is also known as an open deck design, in which the cylinder liners are freestanding in the cylinder case. **RIGHT:** The fourth-generation GSX-R engine was dramatically more compact than its predecessor. A shallower combustion chamber meant that the included valve angles could be reduced, which brought the camshafts closer together for a smaller head. The cam drive moved to the end of the engine, further reducing width.

600
SUZUKI RAM AIR DIRECT
SUZUKI
SUZUKI

Building a Better 600

Suzuki took the opportunity to recenter the 600 class on the new 750's platform, this time expecting considerably more success. It helped greatly that the new bike was much smaller and lighter than the previous 750, so retaining the major (read: expensive) components such as frame, engine, and bodywork made sense.

Introduced in 1997, the GSX-R600 started its development at the same time as the 750; rather than being an afterthought, it was part of the planning for this generation of GSX-Rs. Although it shared a great deal with the 750, the new 600 was destined to be slightly lighter (11 pounds, now 384 dry) and more economical to build. Part of this economy came from the shared components, but other savvy cost-cutting measures were put in place.

Those measures were not specifically in the engine. Sharing the cases with the 750, the 600 nonetheless received a new head atop the revised upper cylinder casting that supported 65.5mm pistons moving through a 44.5mm stroke. The compression ratio was up slightly (12.0 vs. 11.8) compared to the 750, and the valves were, as you'd expect, slightly smaller. The bank of Mikuni carburetors had 36.5mm throats in place of the 750's 39mm units, although they consumed air through a 750-size airbox and ram-air ducts. At the other end, the exhaust system had head pipes 20mm shorter than those on the 750.

OPPOSITE: In conceiving the airflow management of the GSX-R's bodywork, the idea was to make the bike as slippery as possible but not to the extent that the rider would be uncomfortable. To that end, engine cooling was given a lot of thought, with sufficient airflow to keep the engine—and the rider—cool.

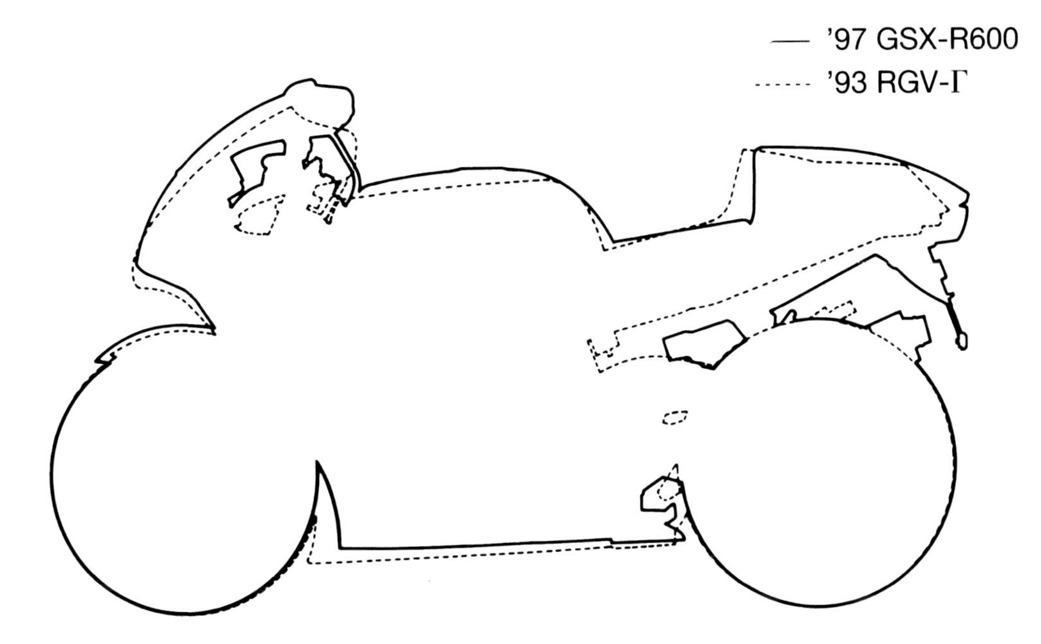

BELOW: This outline comparison speaks volumes about the race-bred direction of the fourth-generation GSX-R. Here it is compared to the 1993 RGV500 Gamma GP race bike. Although the GSX-R is slightly larger (a packaging necessity dictated by the additional ancillary components needed on a street bike), it's not by much. Note that the wheelbase and the rider's position on the bikes are the same.

ABOVE: Mel Harris, vice president of American Suzuki's motorcycle and ATV divisions recalls, "We've been very successful with the GSX-R. The trend was for the GSX-R to be the benchmark. The other companies had to go after it."

Suzuki also debuted direct ignition on the 600, a year ahead of the 750 receiving the same technology. Sometimes known as "stick" coils, each spark plug cap held a small ignition coil, which reduced the length of the high-voltage circuit and improved spark energy. This technology also allowed for individual cylinder timing. Suzuki would turn to mapping each cylinder individually on later GSX-Rs to improve power and throttle response.

Suzuki retained the 750's frame for the 600 but fitted a lighter swingarm without the upper bracing—it wasn't needed on the lighter, lower-power 600—which resulted in a shorter wheelbase of 54.7 inches (0.3 inch shorter than the 750's). In a similar vein, the 750's inverted fork was replaced by a conventional Showa fork, and the six-piston calipers from the 750 gave way to four-pot Tokicos on the 600. Suspension rates were reduced as well.

Those are the specifications. What was important to Suzuki was that it had a competitive 600 class sportbike to uphold the GSX-R name. Road tests hailed the GSX-R's taut chassis and good power. Like the 750, it was considered much more serious, radical even, compared to the 600 class weaponry of the age: Honda's CBR600F3, still aiming for street manners over outright sporting demeanor; Kawasaki's ZX-6R, improving with every generation but still considered "comfortable"; and Yamaha's YZF600R, very much out to be all things to all riders with a near-sport-touring riding position and (still) a steel frame. For pure sporting prowess, nothing was in the GSX-R600's class.

Proof of that came from the racetrack, where the GSX-R600 was competitive immediately. In 1998, Steve Crevier won the AMA Supersport title on a GSX-R600 campaigned by Yoshimura.

More important, particularly to American Suzuki Motor Corporation, by the end of this generation Mat Mladin had taken the AMA Superbike crown on the GSX-R750, ending a ten-year drought. "Racing has always been part of the GSX-R strength, and winning with Mat in '99 was an important outcome for us," says Mel Harris, vice president of the motorcycle/ATV division. "It proved the strength of the bike and without question spurred sales of the streetbike."

These were the earmarks of a company on the move, raising its game in part because it returned to its roots. Those guiding concepts were to make the GSX-R the best-performing bike in the category, to resist diluting that endeavor with compromises for the street rider, and to make the most of its expensive technology by leveraging it across several models. All smart manufacturers are good at spreading the development dollar, but Suzuki, only a fraction the size of Honda, would soon become the industry leader in doing more with less. Suzuki proved that the intelligence of the engineering staff and the drive of the designers matter more than a big R & D budget.

As the fourth generation of GSX-R wound down, few realized that Suzuki had some amazing improvements in store for the GSX-R that would usher in the new millennium.

BELOW LEFT: The GSX-R600's exhaust system, like the 750's, used mild-steel header pipes because they have an excellent balance of weight to cost. Notice the pair of crossover pipes for cylinders two and three; they helped improve midrange response. **BELOW RIGHT:** Stopping power for the 600 came from strong, four-piston calipers gripping 290mm discs. The 750 retained its six-piston calipers, which were considered state of the art when they debuted on the previous-generation 1100. The 600's fork was a conventional slider item to help save weight and reduce costs.

ABOVE LEFT: The double-action rear caliper of the 600—the 750's was the same—helped reduce weight. The locating arm, made out of aluminum, helped transmit braking torque closer to the swingarm pivot. In the years ahead, Suzuki would abandon such a stay to further lower weight. **ABOVE RIGHT:** The 600 and 750 shared Showa suspension components, including a new aluminum-body shock with integral reservoir. Sport riders were by now used to seeing full suspension adjustability, but Suzuki went one better by providing top-grade components.

agv
MOTOREX
SUZUKI
CHEVY TRUCKS
1
YOSHIMURA-RD.COM
GSX
R
SUZUKI
DUNLOP
SUZUKI
elf
DUNLOP

CHAPTER 6

WELCOME BACK TO LITERLAND

Generation 5: 2000–2003

OPPOSITE: Mat Mladin, reigning champion in 2002 aboard the highly developed Yoshimura GSX-R750 racebike, worked harder than ever for results against the newly competitive 1000cc twins. While he gave it his all to earn fifth-and sixth-place finishes at Road Atlanta, he also knew that Suzuki was hard at work preparing the newly launched GSX-R1000 for competition.

Mat Mladin and Yoshimura's success in capturing the AMA Superbike crown in 1999, together with extremely strong sales of both the GSX-R750 and the new, right-size 600, was evidence that Suzuki's engineering staff and market planners made the right decisions in returning to a light, elemental sportbike for the generation that arrived in 1996. Given such success, Suzuki might have chosen to rest, to give the engineers and designers a day or two off and bask in the glory. Many other manufacturers have done so, allowing a groundbreaking product to soldier on with minor updates for several product cycles. The danger in that approach, though, is not just the risk of being overtaken by the competition but also the real possibility that it will cost more to jump back into the fight from a weak position than it would to keep the pressure on.

Suzuki, most emphatically, did not rest. Scarcely halfway through the previous bike's production run, Suzuki began work on the 2000 GSX-R750 with a few simple goals: make it lighter still (having rediscovered the benefits of low mass all over again), make it faster, and make it handle better. Considering the dramatic improvements of the 1996–'99 models over their predecessors, a big leap would not be possible. Already, the GSX-R led the category in high power and low weight, and it didn't look like anyone else was ready to jump back into the 750cc class. Indeed, Kawasaki continued to race the ZX-7R but did not lavish any development on the street version. Yamaha had long since left the class, and Honda remained with only the sport-touring VFR, because the new RC51 was in place for AMA Superbike and World Superbike competition.

With the V-twin TL1000R racing project shelved, Suzuki continued to push the GSX-R750's capabilities for racing for the elite level, as well as to improve chances for the many privateers who campaigned the GSX-R in Supersport and Superstock racing. Even as the market continued to push for a two-class sportbike hierarchy—

BELOW: Mat Mladin rode this Yoshimura Suzuki, based on the 2000 GSX-R750, to four wins and a championship in 2001 (it is shown at Yoshimura's California race shop in spring 2005). Yoshimura chose not to race the new bike in 2000 because development time was tight, and besides, the team had the '99 bike working extremely well. It was a good plan, as Mladin took the first of his five AMA Superbike titles in '99.

LEFT: For Suzuki, the number-one plate reflects the culture of constant improvement and the interaction with race teams that provides valuable input to the production engineers. This environment has allowed the company to close the loop on the racing-improves-the-breed concept in ways that few other manufacturers have managed. This is the tail section from Mat Mladin's 2004 GSX-R1000, carefully packed away at Yoshimura's race shop.

RIGHT: Former GP racer Katsuaki Fujiwara joined the Alstare Suzuki team for the '99 season in World Superbike. The team was new, and Fujiwara was returning from injuries suffered the year before in an off-season GP test; he finished ninth in the standings in 1999 and 2000.

600s and 1000s—the company remained true to the 750. "Many times [the product planners in Japan] asked about the possibility to stop making the 750, but I was firm with them. It is our heritage and we will continue," says Motoo Murakami, executive vice president of American Suzuki and the former head of Suzuki Germany, a key man in developing corporate strategy.

Suzuki's penchant for doing more with less—combining technologies and sharing parts and development time among several motorcycles—was about to rise again. Along with the new GSX-R750 came the predicted GSX-R600 replacement based on the same platform, released a year after the 750 to keep one from stealing the other's marketing push.

There was also a surprise. A big surprise. But we'll get to that later.

As always, Suzuki favored development of the GSX-R750. It's natural. "We produce what we race" is something of a corporate mantra, and at the time AMA Superbike and World Superbike were both in the 750cc fours/1000cc twins format. Suzuki then strove to produce an improved 750 that would also make a competitive 600—no small feat in itself—and that could grow into a world-beating 1000.

But the 750 came first, bristling with new technology. In the search for lower weight and more power—delivered together to make improved performance, as ever—Suzuki revised the chassis, comprehensively reworked the engine, and added a new fuel-injection system that would, once again, cause the other manufacturers to take notice (and, to a great extent, to follow the same technological path). In the end, the new GSX-R became the lightest in the model's history—365 pounds dry, compared to the 395 of the original. And it was the most powerful: while riders were enthralled

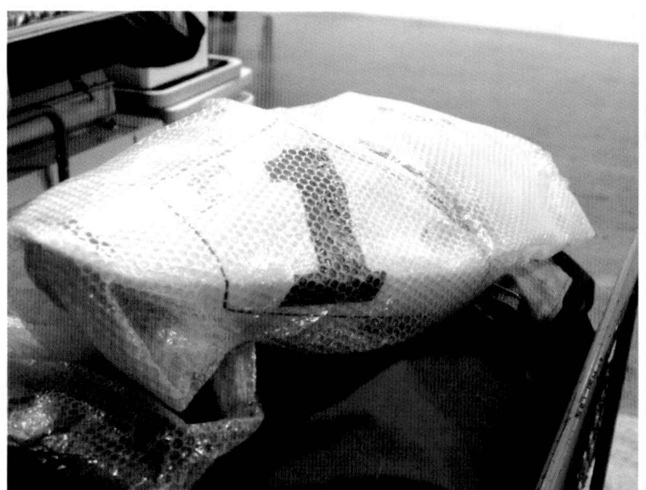

ABOVE LEFT: Frankie Chili, like Mladin, finally got to ride the new-generation GSX-R in 2001. The combination of racing stateside in AMA and continuing to develop the GSX-R through the Alstare team helped Suzuki, in Japan, craft updates for this fifth-generation model. It also helped determine areas to improve for future GSX-Rs. **BELOW LEFT:** The face of the new GSX-R paid homage to the previous bike with twin-reflector headlamps under glass. Now, though, the twin beams were part of a single, lighter assembly that was also more aerodynamic. The big advantage to this layout was the ability to move the leading edges of the enlarged ram-air scoops closer to the center of the fairing for improved efficiency. Suzuki would explore this tactic further in subsequent generations.

ABOVE: Mat Mladin's championship-winning Yoshimura GSX-R750 used the fifth-generation engine and chassis, but it carried forward critical elements from previous years: a sound, well-integrated team; extensive factory support; and the determination to win. Critics said Yoshimura would suffer from the move to a new motorcycle, but instead the team became even more dominant. **ABOVE LEFT:** This was the new face of performance in the early part of the twenty-first century. Suzuki launched an all-new GSX-R750 in 2000 and quickly followed up with a fresh 600 and the astoundingly fast 1000 (shown). Together, the GSX-Rs would dominate sportbiking and reset the expectations of power for displacement and lightness in class. **BELOW LEFT:** Stephane Chambon partnered with Chili at Alstare Suzuki in 2001, eventually finishing twelfth for the season. His more experienced teammate ranked seventh, with a win and two podiums.

M. OKHMURA

with the 1999's 114 horsepower at the rear wheel, the 2000 model was better by 10 hp. *Bam*! Just like that.

Starting with the chassis, Suzuki once again tried to compact the motorcycle. (In fact, with some hindsight we can see this trend, which started with the '96 model, continue to play out. Each generation since the '96 had become smaller, lighter, more efficiently packaged. Even the 1000.) The 2000 model was nearly an inch shorter overall and a quarter inch narrower. The frame, though similar in appearance, was completely revised. It was shorter—the vertical distance from the bottom of the steering head to the swingarm pivot was reduced half an inch, while that measurement horizontally was trimmed 0.3 inch. The height of the stamped-aluminum main spar was reduced 0.3 inch, as well. Components were juggled; the crosspiece below the swingarm pivot that holds the lower shock mount was changed from an extrusion to a casting to save weight, which was partially offset by a new cross brace between the vertical ears supporting the subframe and internal bracing between the massive swingarm-pivot casting and the main side spars. The overall goal was increased rigidity, better crash tolerance, and reduced weight. Overall, the frame changes helped cut 4.4 pounds.

Suzuki's racing success with the GSX-R750 and broad customer acceptance caused the engineers to stick with the previous bike's general chassis dimensions. Rake remained at 24 degrees and trail at 3.8 inches, but the wheelbase grew 0.6 inch thanks to a longer swingarm that itself was significantly reworked. Still braced, the massive forward deck was slimmed, while the lower cross bracing just

OPPOSITE: Suzuki's styling department tried out several themes for the 2000 GSX-R750, including many variations on the dual-headlight theme. The many options considered show how far afield Suzuki's stylists were willing to search for that rare blend of GSX-R family resemblance and the much-desired "new model" look.

BELOW: This side-view illustration shows a considerably more radical and angular GSX-R than the one eventually built. Suzuki felt, at this point in the GSX-R's life, that some linkage to the previous model was necessary—particularly because the '96–'99 bikes had been not just a sales success but a racing success as well.

ABOVE: The GSX-R750 development team, from left to right: Hiromi Deguchi (engine development), Akihiko Muramatsu (planning), Yukihiro Takasaki (electrical—EFI), Kunio Arase (project leader), Yukihisa Hirasawa (service), Akimasa Hatanaka (chassis development), Hisayuki Sugita (chassis engineer—setup), and Yuichi Nakashima (test rider).

in front of the tire was increased in size. A new aluminum-body shock from Showa saved a pound all by itself despite having a larger, 46mm damping piston. It's not everyday that you get a better piece—improved damping and durability—and have it weigh less, too.

Up front, the GSX-R750's Showa fork was revised, with more travel but less overall length, and placed in triple clamps 0.3 inch (7mm) narrower. The top stem nut was changed from steel to aluminum. Bolting to this inverted fork were new brake components, a step back to four-piston calipers from the '99's six-piston versions. Together with lighter front discs, the brakes alone were responsible for nearly 2 pounds of lost weight. (The rear brake received an aluminum piston for reduced weight.) Even the wheels came in for scrutiny: new, diamond-shaped spokes, a smaller 5.5-inch rear wheel wearing the now-standard 180-cross-section tire, and a redesigned sprocket/cush-drive setup slashed 3 pounds from the bike.

The new bodywork—clearly still a GSX-R but usefully modernized—also contributed to the weight-loss program. The fairing panels were thinner (2mm vs. 2.5 on the '99) with fewer parts. The twin-bulb headlight assembly used a single reflector and saved weight over the 1999s, and it moved the leading edge of the ram-air ducts closer to the center of the bike, for improved efficiency. Here again you can see Suzuki's wind-tunnel work arriving in the showroom.

Moving on to the engine: you could be excused for assuming, at a glance, that the 2000 bike's engine was a carryover item. In fact, it was almost completely new. Retaining the double-split crankcase—the crankshaft and transmission shafts are carried on two planes—the 2000 engine's bottom end was reworked to move the transmission shafts closer to the crank for an overall reduction in engine length. The upper part of the crankcase, which had been two pieces in the previous 600 and 750, was now one, following what had become industry convention. With this change, Suzuki deleted an external hose that provided oil to the top end and replaced it with an internal gallery, saving weight. Although the engine retained the previous 72mm-by-46mm bore and stroke, the pistons were forged instead of cast aluminum (thus lighter and stronger), and the wrist pins had tapered bores for yet more weight reduction.

Lighter pistons permit lighter components down the line; the connecting rods (now shot-peened for strength) were thinner and gripped 1mm-thinner main journals. The crank was reduced in size a millimeter here and a millimeter there.

Even the cams came in for a weight reduction, with a larger inner diameter. They rode in a new head with reduced valve angles—now 25 degrees compared to 29 for the '99 bike—for a more compact combustion chamber and straighter intake ports. The valves remained the same size but were closed by single springs for 2000 and had thinner stems. By careful development of the head layout, it was no taller than before. Slightly smaller chambers netted an increase in compression ratio to 12.0:1 (up from 11.8:1). A side note on the head design: it now carried internal passages for the PAIR (pulsed air injection) emissions system. Before, external lines led to flanges just above the exhaust port on bikes built for certain markets, such as California. But with emissions regulations becoming stricter, all bikes would need some kind of air injection. To simplify hardware and save weight overall, Suzuki made the change to the head casting. It slightly complicated the casting and machining of the head, but it simplified the number of external components and reduced assembly time.

All of these engine changes may seem minor in terms of producing horsepower, but they contributed to the whole and allowed maximum advantage to come from the GSX-R's improved induction and exhaust systems. The all-stainless four-into-two-into-one exhaust system wasn't much different except for a shorter muffler. But the injection system was all new.

"I was originally told that this idea was not good and not to pursue it," says Kunio Arase of his concept for the GSX-R's unique twin-throttle-valve injection system. "But I felt it was a good idea, so I continued to work on it in my spare time and on weekends." Good thing he did. At its introduction, the GSX-R's new injection was lauded as a great step forward, making electronic injection feel more like a set of well-calibrated carburetors. (Many riders disliked the instantaneous response of modern injection, which could really upset the chassis during hard riding, particularly with a high-performance, light-flywheel engine.)

OPPOSITE: Among the improvements to the GSX-R750 for 2000 was a new fuel-injection system fed by a larger, freer-breathing airbox. The slots cut into the velocity stacks inside the airbox were an advanced part of the design, helping manage airflow during high-rpm operation and smoothing the torque curve.

The key to this system was in maintaining good air velocity in the intake ports. With traditional single-throttle injection, when the rider whacks open the throttle the air can nearly stagnate, causing a stumble. The slide on constant-velocity carburetors was designed to prevent this condition by partly blocking the intake tract and maintaining good velocity. But CV carbs can only react to intake flow, and they can sometimes be fooled. Jetting was a fine art.

In Suzuki's new system the secondary throttle valve resides just upstream of the rider-controlled throttle. The engine-control unit manages it with settings based on dyno testing. It cannot be fooled. At the same time, the throttle bodies were revised with slightly larger outlets (on the engine side) and inlets (near the airbox) but slightly smaller (42mm vs. 46mm) throttle plates. The injectors were re-aimed to set at 60 degrees from the main throttle-body axis instead of 32 degrees, so that the fuel spray hit the wide-open throttle plate at maximum power to help promote atomization of the fuel. Before, the fuel did not come into contact with the throttle plate.

This double-throttle system was managed by a new, lighter (of course), more powerful computer that held eight distinct injection maps—two for each cylinder, one for light load, and one for heavy load. The computer decided which to use based on throttle position, engine rpm, intake vacuum, and other parameters. At light load, the computer read the intake vacuum for a more precise indication of throttle position. At high load, it excluded this input and relied on throttle position and rpm. The system also took into account vehicle speed, ambient pressure, coolant temperature (mainly for cold starting), and cues from the sidestand and tip-over switches.

A new airbox fed this system, as well. The secondary throttle plates had the added benefit of reducing intake noise—especially during the official emissions tests—so the flapper valve used in the '99 model could be eliminated. (More weight savings.) The GSX-R also regained its renowned intake honk.

When you think about the state of affairs in 2000, it's still amazing that Suzuki lavished so much effort on the 750, even if you knew a reworked 600 was coming. In any event, the new 750 sparked a new round of appreciation for the class.

"I don't mean to take anything away from the original GSX-R750," explains Paul Dean, editorial director of *Cycle World* magazine. "But the 2000 model just got everything right. It was fast, great handling, and gave me tremendous confidence. I think that bike was a true high point of the 750's development."

"The 2000 model was a major surprise, given that all the other manufacturers had basically left the 750 class," says Kent Kunitsugu, editor of *Sport Rider*. "The jump in performance was almost as great as the '96 model's progression, which surely took a lot of R & D resources that other compa-

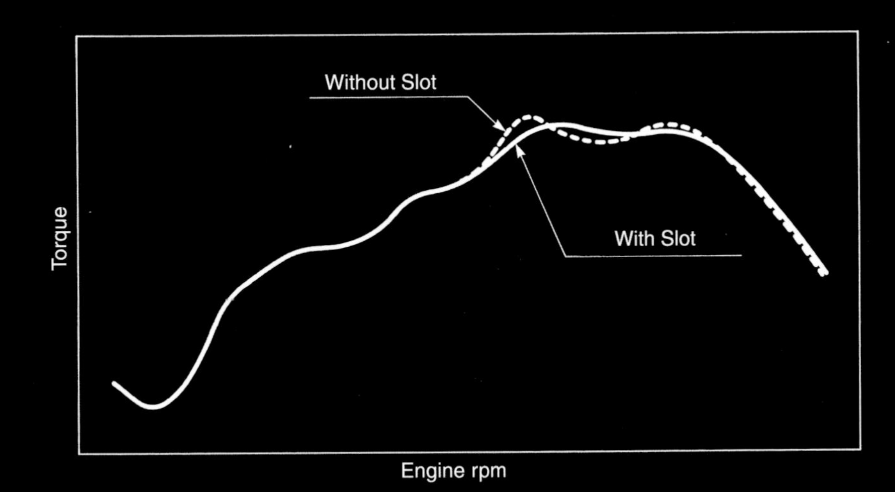
Without Slot
With Slot
Torque
Engine rpm

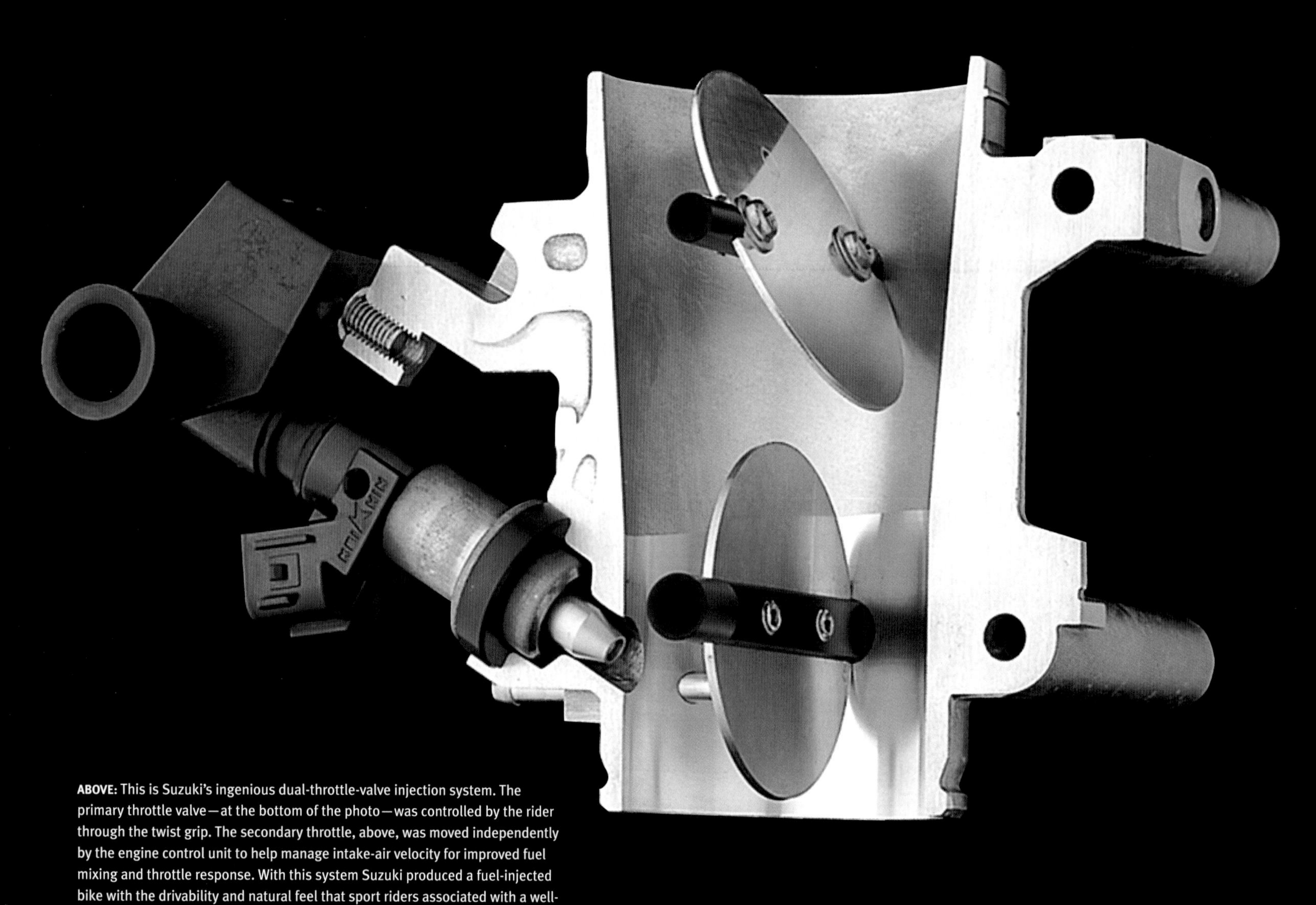

ABOVE: This is Suzuki's ingenious dual-throttle-valve injection system. The primary throttle valve—at the bottom of the photo—was controlled by the rider through the twist grip. The secondary throttle, above, was moved independently by the engine control unit to help manage intake-air velocity for improved fuel mixing and throttle response. With this system Suzuki produced a fuel-injected bike with the drivability and natural feel that sport riders associated with a well-jetted carbureted model.

BELOW: It wasn't just the addition of the second throttle valve that made the SDTV—Suzuki dual throttle valve—injection unique. It was also the specific angle of the injector and the length of the throttle body itself. Despite having more components in the stream, the new dual-valve setup was actually shorter.

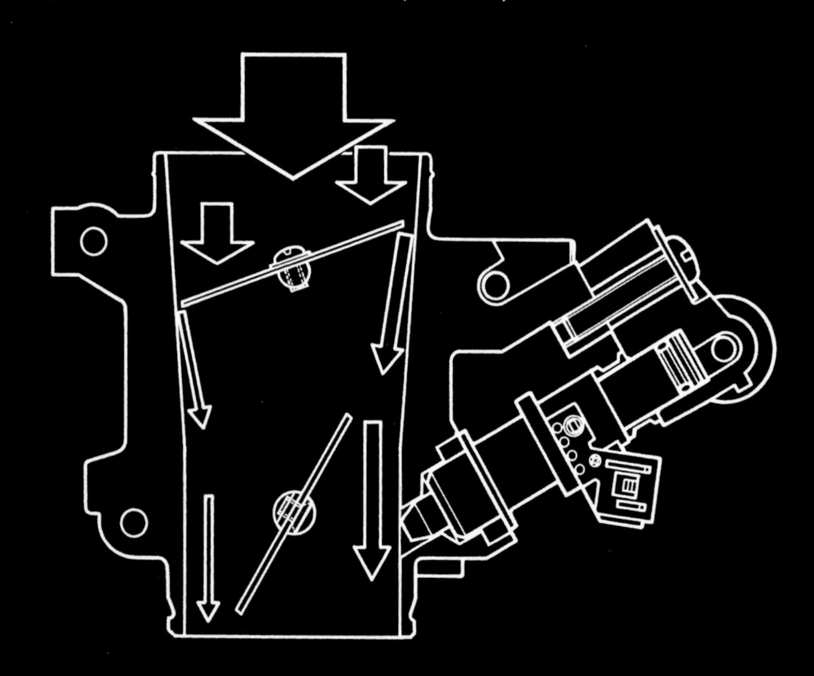

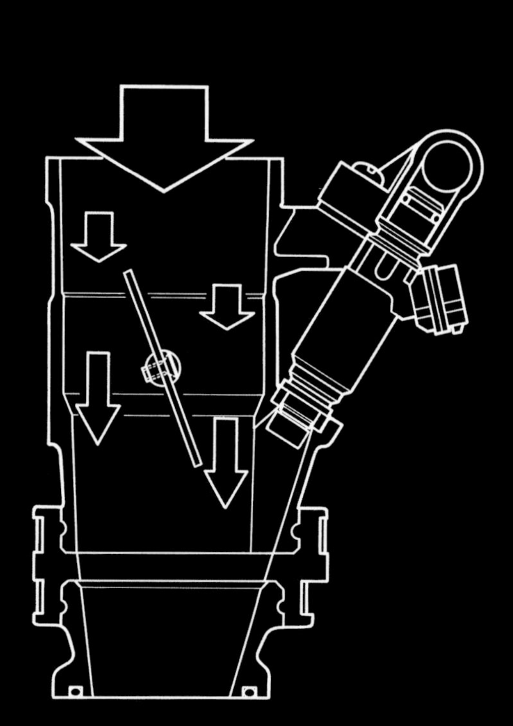

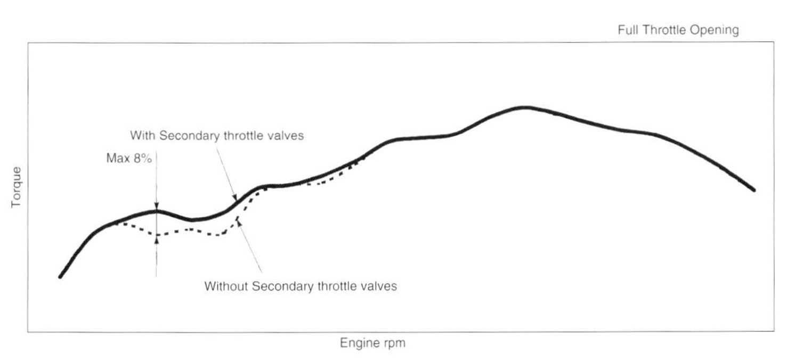

Torque Improvement by Secondary Throttle Valves

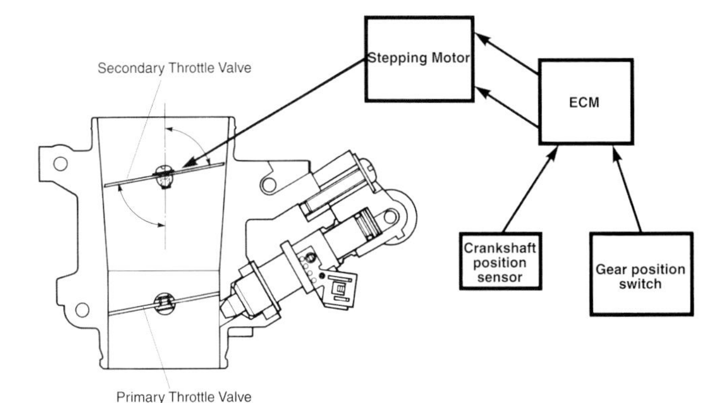

nies would have diverted to 'more important' (read: 'better selling') models. It's pretty obvious that the GSX-R750 is a matter of corporate pride to Suzuki. But for good reason: they are justifiably proud of the fact that the original GSX-R750 was the bike that started the 'racer-replica' revolution."

In its first year, the fifth-generation GSX-R was as strongly praised as the original. It won numerous bike-of-the-year awards and often placed extremely well in competition with open-class machines. *Motorcyclist* magazine named the GSX-R750 the Motorcycle of the Year in 2000. It won *Cycle World*'s Best Superbike award that year as well. When tossed into comparisons looking for ultimate handling and performance, it usually won outright.

Mat Mladin took the AMA Superbike crown again in 2000—albeit on the 1999 bike because the new model had not arrived in time for necessary testing before the season began. Once again, Suzukis dominated the stock classes and were the bike of choice for privateers.

And yet there was more to come.

The New 600

Suzuki performed the same engineering feats with the 2001 GSX-R600 as it had with the '97, heavily basing it off thc 750 of the same generation. It worked, again.

ABOVE LEFT: The benefits of the dual throttle valves were experienced primarily at the low end of the rpm spread, with a maximum of 8 percent more torque near the bottom of the band. This was because the secondary throttle valves limited air intake to preserve velocity at low revs. The throttles thus could be sized larger to pass sufficient air for maximum high-rpm power.

ABOVE RIGHT: The control scheme for the SDTV used an extra map built into the ECU to determine the opening size and rate, dependent on engine rpm; throttle position; and a host of secondary factors, including air temperature and density.

LEFT: For 2001, Suzuki introduced the third generation of GSX-R600. Based, again, on the 750, this time it shared all bodywork components so that they were essentially the same size. However, extensive weight-saving measures in the engine and frame (strategically thinner-gauge aluminum in the frame, for example) helped make the 600 usefully lighter than the 750. It was also the first 600cc machine to achieve the landmark output of 100 hp at the rear wheel.

LEFT: The 2000 GSX-R750 engine took the split-crankcase design one step further by integrating the cylinder block and the upper crankcase. Casting techniques were developed at Suzuki that allowed this part to be manufactured according to desirably tighter tolerances with excellent repeatability. As a result, the new engine was lighter, yet more powerful, than before.

RIGHT: The GSX-R750's braced swingarm was constructed of cast, stamped, and extruded elements. It was strong enough to be used on the still-to-come 1000cc machine with minor modifications. Suffice it to say, it was plenty robust for the 750 at street speeds.

For 2001, the third generation of GSX-R600 arrived, though it was almost overshadowed by the introduction of the 1000. The 600 was a virtual clone of the 750—same bodywork, seat, wheels, brakes, and general layout. The frame was very similar to the 750's, but it was lightened in places to match the lower output of the engine. The fork remained a conventional Showa cartridge unit but was given the same weight-saving process that was afforded to the 750's upside-down fork. The swingarm was derived from the old bike's, again without the bracing of the 750's, and it was 20mm longer than the previous 600's. New four-piston front brakes were lighter as well; the old 600 never got the six-piston Tokicos of the 750. In other words, all the hard work that went into the 2000 GSX-R750 was, by duplication, put into the 600.

However, the engine was significantly different. Since Suzuki had gone to the new single-piece cylinder block/upper crankcase casting, a new casting had to be created for the 67mm-by-42.5mm bore and stroke. The block was slightly shorter, and the head, though the same width and length as the 750's (which facilitated sharing parts), was different. The valve angles were slightly wider—28 degrees to the 750's 25—and the intake ports weren't quite as vertical. The compression ratio was slightly higher, at 12.2:1. Below, the 600's components were incrementally downsized from the 750's but shared the architecture.

On the dyno, the new 600 broke the magical 100 hp mark for 600s, if only by a little. It was the second bike to wear fuel injection in the 600 class—after the ill-fated Triumph TT600—and the first to break 100 hp. The GSX-R600 staked its claim.

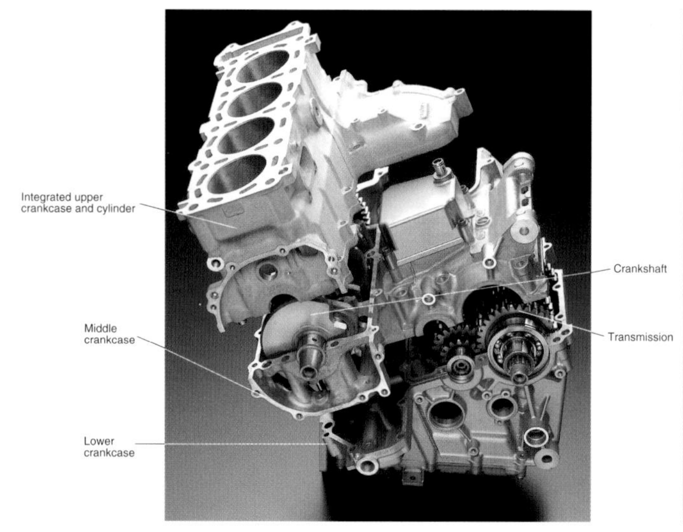

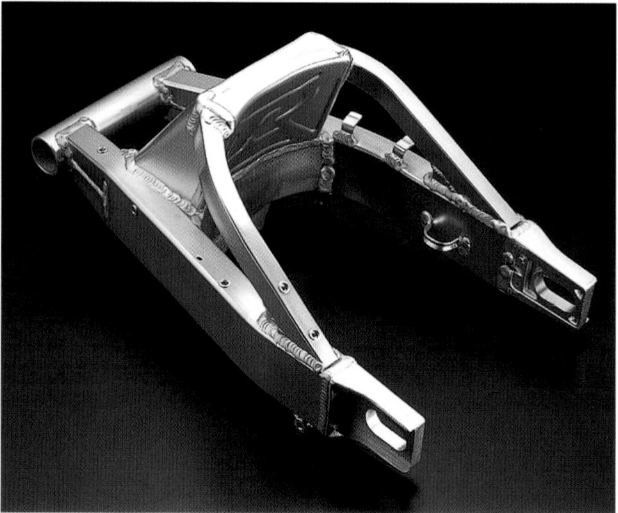

Dropping the Big One

Members of the press and enthusiasts had expected Suzuki to rejoin the open class. It just had to. By 2000, Honda had an uprated version of the CBR929RR, Yamaha continued to refine the YZF-R1—a bike thought by many to be the most significant model in this new generation of light-is-right sportbikes to follow in the wheel tracks of the original GSX-R—and Kawasaki gamely kept the ZX-9R on the development track.

You can imagine the debate inside Suzuki. The GSX-R750 placed extremely well in many Superbike shootouts of the period, partly because its mighty engine produced nearly the same peak power as the Honda's. Why develop a new 1000cc model when the 750 was doing just fine?

It's unlikely the debate lasted long, however. The other liter bikes were selling quite well at a reasonable profit margin for the other manufacturers. And at the same time the 1000cc V-twins were running away with AMA Superbike and World Superbike racing, the push was beginning from inside those sanctioning bodies to switch to 1000cc fours for racing.

In addition, Suzuki was not content to watch a reenactment of the Honda-Yamaha war without

ABOVE: The GSX-R1000 kept the clean lines of the 750 and 600. Even the color scheme, though not identical to the 750's or the 600's, was similar enough to create something of an understated, near-stealth appearance for the 1000.

FAR LEFT: A thoroughly revised rear suspension system used a Showa integral-reservoir shock with full adjustability. Suzuki also retained a threaded fork at the top shock mount to facilitate changes in ride height without altering spring preload. A race kit from the company provided the necessary shims, but the aftermarket also filled this demand. **LEFT:** All three GSX-Rs in this generation received new, lighter wheels and rear brake calipers with aluminum pistons. No part had gone unnoticed in the quest for reduced weight. Every opportunity the engineers took to reduce weight—especially unsprung weight—was cause for celebration.

RIGHT: From the front, the main differences between the GSX-R1000 and the 750 were the 1000's gold-colored fork tubes and the six-piston front brakes. There were other, much more subtle cues—such as the slightly larger lower fairing—but Suzuki played the conservative styling card with the 1000. Once again, the parts-sharing scheme permitted the company to produce the three models for much less than the cost of developing three uniquely individual GSX-Rs.

jumping into the fight. The result was the universally lauded GSX-R1000. From the start, the big GSX-R dominated, producing 142 rear-wheel horsepower to the Yamaha's 130. It was light, astoundingly fast, and yet as docile as such a high-performance motorcycle could be.

When the early press materials arrived, some were surprised that it didn't look a lot different than the 600 and 750. Indeed, from perusing the specifications, you'd think it was little more than a tweaked 750. These first impressions couldn't have been more off the mark.

It's true, however, that Suzuki heavily leveraged the 750 to create the 1000. The frame was essentially the same, as was the majority of the bodywork (the lower fairing was slightly different). By altering materials in the alloy frame, the GSX-R1000's unit was 6 percent stiffer than the 750's; the swingarm was stiffened by 1 percent. Nothing major, in other words.

Two of the prominent visual cues were the wider rear tire—a 190/50VR17 on a 6.0-inch-wide rim—and the gold-colored fork tubes. Suzuki turned to Kayaba for a new fork finish to reduce seal friction (sometimes called *stiction*) and got back an inverted fork with a titanium-nitride finish. While the fork has your attention, perhaps you'll notice the six-piston brakes in place of the 750's four-pot units. Still, from five steps back the GSX-R1000 didn't seem to be much more than a big-bore 750.

Again, the assessment understates the reality. As soon as press bikes started to hit the dyno, the world of open-class street bikes was turned on its head. Most competitors were turning out 125 to 130 hp at the rear wheel, but the 2001 GSX-R1000 pounded out around 143. This was not an incremental improvement but rather a showstopping, tire-screeching change in direction. The horsepower wars were over before the others could so much as cough.

Perhaps most impressive about the 2001 GSX-R1000's power dominance is that it came from an engine virtually identical to the 750's and, according to most tuners, in a fairly mild state of tune. Suzuki chose to use as much of the 750 as possible, so the 1000's bore increase was limited to 1mm. The rest of the boost to 988cc would have to come from stroke, which traditionally benefits torque production more than an increase in peak power. The 1000's 59mm stroke was the longest in the class in 2001. What's more, Suzuki had the audacity to use the 750's cylinder head essentially unchanged. Common wisdom was that valves ideal for a 750 would be prohibitively small for a 1000.

Even the intake system was borrowed straight from the 750, with some minor changes and the requisite computer reprogramming. The servo that controlled the secondary throttle body was now mounted right to the throttle-body rack, not remotely as before. This change would come to the 750 in 2002 along with an extremely clever fast-idle system. Before, there had been a small lever on the handlebar to raise the idle speed for starting. The new system—arriving across the board in 2002—used a small cam mounted to the secondary throttle shaft to open the primary throttle slightly. It did this by forcing

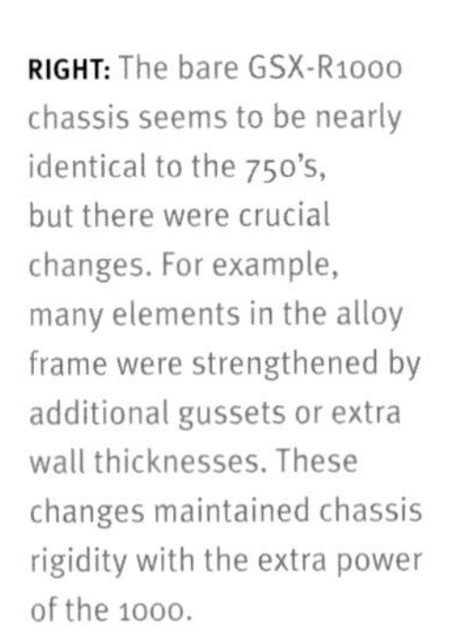

RIGHT: The bare GSX-R1000 chassis seems to be nearly identical to the 750's, but there were crucial changes. For example, many elements in the alloy frame were strengthened by additional gussets or extra wall thicknesses. These changes maintained chassis rigidity with the extra power of the 1000.

BELOW LEFT: A new electronic instrument panel debuted with this generation of GSX-R. A stepper-motor tachometer—a thin electric motor moved the needle—took center stage. All the lighting was by LED for low power consumption and excellent longevity.

BELOW RIGHT: Suzuki's masterstroke with the 1000 was the implementation of a gear-driven counterbalancer. Long-stroke, large-displacement inline-fours can have unacceptable levels of vibration, but the counterbalancer offered an opposing force that effectively eliminated the vibration. From there, the benefits accrued, as the rest of the motorcycle could be lighter when not subjected to vibration.

the secondary throttle valve slightly over center. As soon as the rider opened the throttle, the secondary system could return to its partially closed state to manage airflow. As the engine warmed, the secondary system returned to normal operation.

Suzuki didn't pull out the engineering stops to achieve its class-leading peak power, suggesting that Suzuki either had modest ambitions for the 1000 or—as it turns out was more the case—it was sandbagging, keeping a bit in reserve until its competitors responded. That isn't to say the GSX-R1000's engine didn't have some tricks of its own. Increased heat output made a traditional oil cooler necessary, fitted to the chin fairing. The 73mm pistons were, amazingly, even lighter than the 750's 72mm slugs.

Changes were made to the upper and central crankcase castings for two reasons. One was to accommodate the 13mm-longer stroke. The other was to introduce a technology to the sportbike class that would have a great impact on the bike's demeanor: a crank-driven counterbalancer.

When an inline-four gets to a certain size, vibration can become a big issue, both for component longevity and for rider comfort. Suzuki developed a simple counterbalancer positioned on the crankshaft split line and hung out in front of the engine. In theory, this was not the most effective place for a balancer, but it was offset by the fact that it was up out of the oil supply, which reduced

BELOW LEFT: The GSX-R1000 engine was a marvel of modern engineering. Amazingly light, compact, and durable, it reset the standards for the class. What's more, it achieved all of this without the technological gimmicks other manufacturers had followed (often into dead ends). Rather, the 988cc engine was extremely well developed—in part on the dyno at Ryuyo and in part on the racetrack, through experience with AMA and World Superbike racing. **BELOW RIGHT:** Amazingly, the new 1000's engine was just 15mm taller than the 750's and because the bore was only 1mm larger (at 73mm), the engine was no wider. Careful attention to component weights—the pistons and connecting rods were lighter than the 750's—kept the overall weight in check. In all, the 1000 was a hugely potent yet comparatively tiny engine.

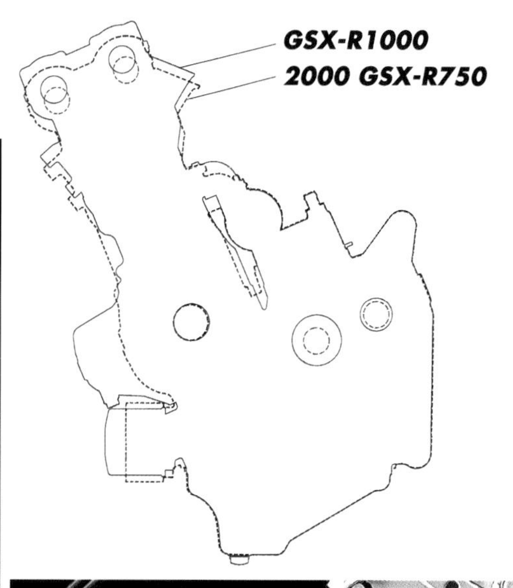

RIGHT: Compare the GSX-R600's crankshaft (below) to the 1000's (above). The larger engine has, of course, more stroke, but the other giveaway is the second gear placed on the number-two cylinder's left cheek. This gear drives the case-mounted counterbalancer. **FAR RIGHT:** The 1000's cylinder head was essentially the same unit as the one used on the 750, including valve sizes and angles. The comparatively small valves improved low-end torque but, fortunately, still flowed well enough to permit a massive top-end wallop. The eccentric cam on the fuel injection (top of photo) helped soften the partial-throttle response of this very torquey engine.

LEFT, BELOW LEFT, AND BELOW RIGHT: Suzuki created a simplified exhaust tuning technology—called SET (Suzuki exhaust tuning)—that was a butterfly valve in the lead-in pipe, just before the muffler. It was controlled by an electric servo and operated by a pair of cables. It was straightforward, robust, and effective: torque improved by 6 percent at low rpm.

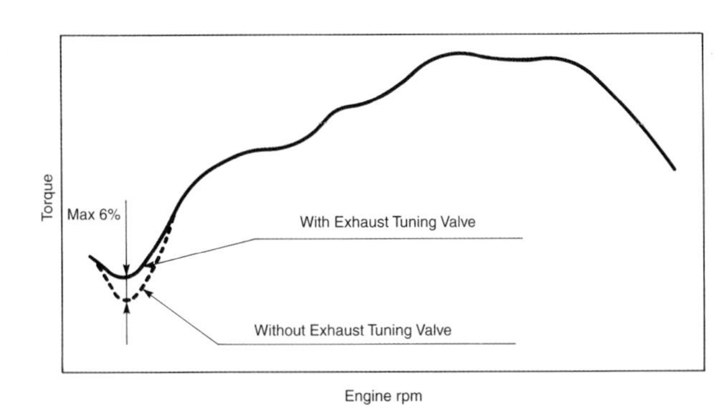

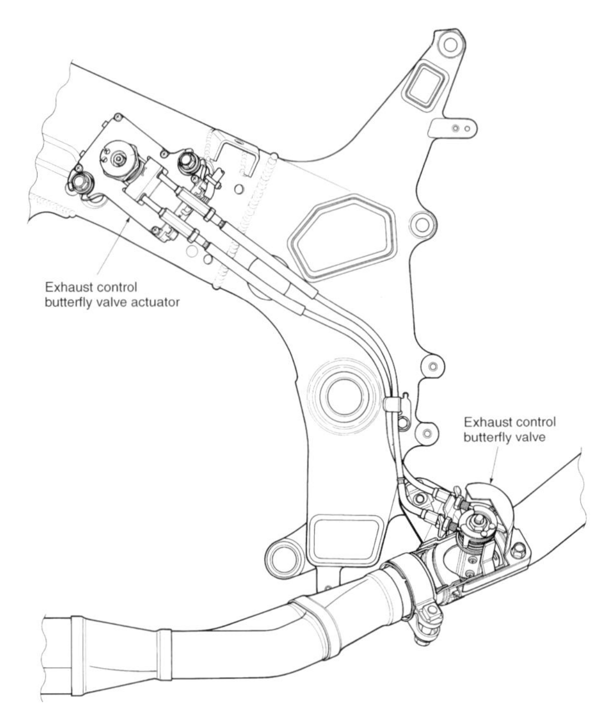

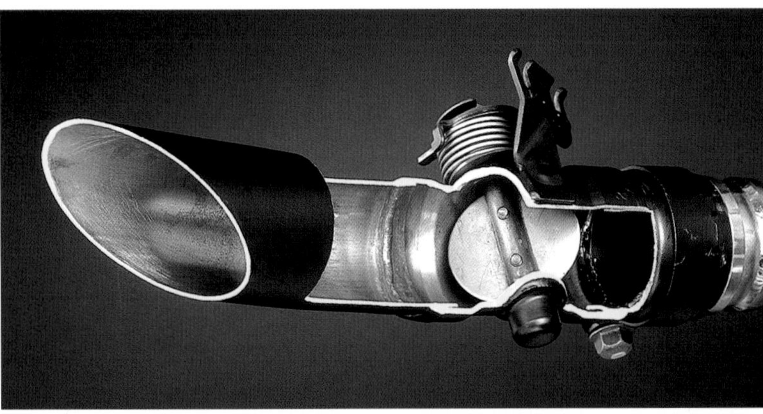

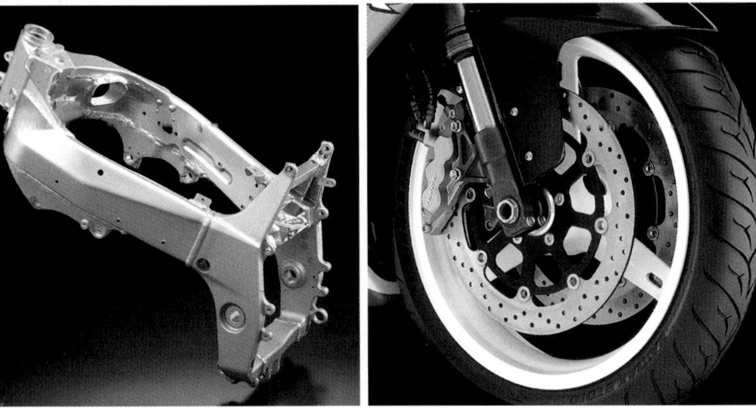

ABOVE LEFT: Suzuki's fifth-generation GSX-R frame borrowed little from the frame of the original model, except perhaps the governing concept: be strong yet light. For the 1000, as on the 600 and 750, this was achieved through a combination of castings (steering head and swingarm pivot area) and stampings (in the main beams). Even a few extruded pieces were chosen for this specific kind of strength. **ABOVE RIGHT:** To accommodate the high speeds predicted for the 1000, a set of six-piston calipers gripped floating 310mm rotors. The Kayaba fork's titanium-nitride finish reduced friction for an improved ride, and the 1000 had higher spring and damping rates compared to the 750. **RIGHT:** Kayaba (KYB) also supplied the 1000's rear suspension. The integral-reservoir shock had an aluminum body and comprehensive adjustability. The 1000 carried a 6-inch-wide rear wheel wearing a 190mm-wide tire that Bridgestone developed specifically for this bike's performance characteristics.

ABOVE: And then there were three. By the end of 2002, Suzuki had thoroughly developed the GSX-R into a winning platform in 600cc, 750cc, and 1000cc displacements. It was a winner on the racetrack and comprehensively so in magazine comparisons and road tests.

windage drag. Suzuki's engineers worked extremely hard to reduce the weight impact of the balancer shaft as well as any power losses associated with it. As such, it ran on plain metal bearings and was gear driven from teeth cut into a crank balance weight.

The primary benefit of the counterbalancer is the GSX-R's uncanny smoothness. Most liter bikes of the period were built with low weight in mind, so the engines had become solidly mounted to the frame. Some vibrated intensely at certain engine speeds. Throughout the rev range, particularly in the midrange cruising speeds, the GSX-R1000 was eerily serene. The combination of the GSX-R1000's incredible top-end rip and its meaty midrange—better than all its competitors'—gave the bike exemplary flexibility.

"We can thank the 2001 GSX-R1000 for the unbelievable state of liter bike performance we enjoy now," comments Kent Kunitsugu, *Sport Rider* editor. "All of the open-class machines previous had street bike compromises in their design; the '01 model basically took the gloves off and laid down the gauntlet that others have had trouble responding to ever since."

To say the GSX-R1000 changed the face of liter bike performance is a raw, almost egregious understatement. For 2001 and 2002, it was the undisputed king of the class. Yamaha gave the R1 a mighty shove up the performance ladder but couldn't reach the GSX-R. Honda immediately moved up development of the CBR929RR and created the stopgap CBR954RR. Kawasaki all but gave up with the ZX-9R. In fact, it would take until 2004 before the competing manufacturers could mount a serious challenge to the GSX-R1000's utter and complete dominance of the class. But by then it was nearly too late for them. More improvements, more racing experience, and more development were in store for every GSX-R on the menu.

SUZUK

CHAPTER 7

THE 1000 TAKES THE LEAD

Generation 6: 2003–2005

OPPOSITE: With the striking 2003 GSX-R1000, Suzuki left no impression unaltered. The goal was to marry the head-of-the-pack performance that made the GSX-R1000 famous with a newfound, slightly edgier style. The styling department was issued the mandate: Make the new liter bike compelling and distinctive.

BELOW: At the Suzuki headquarters in Hamamatsu, Hiroaki Chosa explains his design influences to publisher David Bull (one of these influences happens to be the fighter jets he sees taking off and landing every morning on his ride to work). The youthful styling designer is typical of those working on the latest GSX-Rs: enthusiastic, charismatic, and above all, a rider.

The launch of the sixth generation of GSX-R marked a shift in Suzuki's emphasis on two fronts. One, the GSX-R1000 now took the upper hand in the development stakes. Historically, the 750 led the march—arriving first, gaining the most recent technology, absorbing the lion's share of corporate pride—but by 2003 the 1000 was in the lead. Two, the GSX-R1000 represents another, more subtle shift for Suzuki engineering, in which the designers—the lucky guys who get to clothe these amazing machines—have more freedom of expression. With this generation, the designs turned edgier, sharper, more aggressive looking than ever.

What's more, the 2003 GSX-R1000 would be the proving ground for a host of changes brought to the GSX-R600 and 750 for 2004. In fact, nearly every upgrade to the smaller bikes appeared on the 1000 a year before.

But the real impetus for driving the GSX-R1000 to the head of development and, indeed, shortening its development cycle was competition both on the track and in the showroom. For the track, it was understood that Superbike racing would revert to allowing 1000cc four-cylinder bikes in place of the 750s that had been the limit since 1982. In 2002, Yoshimura and Mat Mladin barely lost the AMA Superbike crown to Nicky Hayden aboard the Honda RC51. But it would be the RC's swan song of competitiveness with the change to 1000cc fours. To keep speeds in check, the AMA Superbike rules would require 1000cc fours to have some additional limitations compared to the twins and triples. For example, "Cylinder heads may be ported and machined, but altering of valve angles will not be permitted; aftermarket valves, springs, retainers, and other valve-train components will be permitted; valves must be stock size and same basic material as original equipment; aftermarket camshafts will be permitted, but cam lift and resulting valve lift must be no greater than stock." In addition, the "stock crankshaft

LEFT: When it debuted in late 2002, the revised GSX-R indicated Suzuki's styling trends for the next few years, though few enthusiasts knew that at the time. It was more rakish and purposeful, and more to the point, it looked distinctly different from the 600 and 750 for the first time in its short history.

RIGHT: Again, early design studies reveal interesting themes, some of which you can clearly see on the production version. The vents in the tail section help break up the surface and add visual excitement. Notice also how the passenger footpegs were to be mounted with vertical hardware. This study also depicts a different way of mounting the rear subframe, with the upper mounts hidden beneath the forward edge of the saddle.

must be retained. The only allowable modifications are balancing, polishing of bearing surfaces and attachment of accessory drives. Homologated transmission gear sets (one optional set of ratios per approved model) will be permitted. Optional sets will be price-controlled and must be available to any legitimate AMA Superbike competitor. Homologated fuel-injection throttle-body assemblies (one optional type per approved model) and aftermarket airboxes will be permitted. Modifications to throttle bodies will not be permitted. Optional throttle bodies will be price-controlled and must be available to any legitimate AMA Superbike competitor."

The thinking was simple: keep the liter bikes from sucking through massive throttle bodies, and the horsepower might not (and, it was hoped, would not) go through the roof.

In preparation for racing, Suzuki wanted to make a host of small changes to the GSX-R1000, but its motivation was also to keep the bike at the forefront of open-class street bikes. Suzuki engineers knew that Honda and Kawasaki were readying all-new models—the CBR954RR and the ZX-9R had long since been vanquished—and rumor had it that Yamaha was ready with yet another push with the R1.

It was the right time to make alterations to the 1000.

Heading the list was, as one might expect, a revised engine. Despite the fact that the engine was already the strongest in the class by a healthy margin—all without moving from the original 988cc displacement—it received significant alterations. From the cam cover to the crankshaft, the engine is the same as the original 2001–2002 GSX-R1000's, with a slightly longish stroke and modest bore, plus a gear-driven counterbalancer at crankshaft level to reduce vibration.

But for the 2003 model, Suzuki aimed to reduce friction and internal losses, so a set of ports was let into the crank webs between the cylinders. The concept here was that as one piston rushed down from top-dead center, the air in the crankcase below it had to have someplace to go. Traditionally, the trapped air would migrate downward into the oil pan but not without exerting a slight bit of force on the bottom of the pistons. It was pumping loss, a form of drag and a consumer of precious horsepower. But for the '03 engine, portals were machined into the bottom of the cylin-

BELOW: Looking forward. The more angular lines of the 2003 GSX-R1000 were already influencing future product, as these early design sketches for the 2004 GSX-R600 and 750 will attest. Even so, the decision had been made to keep the 1000 and the 600/750 models on a slightly different stylistic path, maintaining familial resemblances while also retaining the 1000's distinct identity.

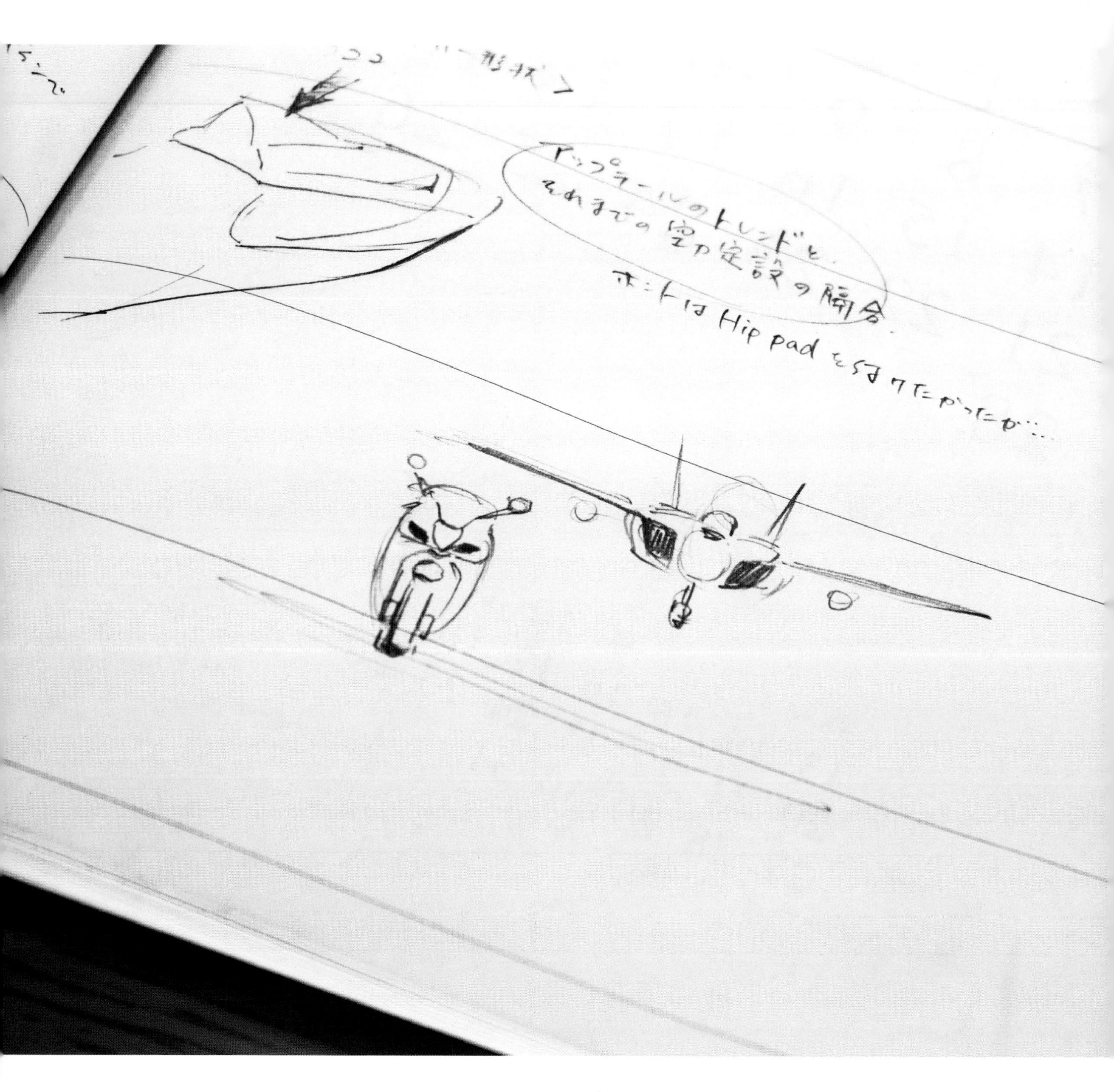
アップテールのトレンドと、
それまでの空力定説の融合。
ホントはHip padを付けたかったが…

OPPOSITE AND LEFT: Mr. Chosa and his doodles. He was inspired by the look of fighter aircraft, and it's possible to see the influence of the F/A-22 in the shape of the GSX-R1000's ram-air scoops.

der bore between bottom-dead center and the top of the main-bearing saddle. They allowed crankcase pressure to migrate freely between the cylinders. Other minor changes included an internal oil passage for the hydraulic cam-chain tensioner.

Suzuki then turned its attention to the induction system, switching from individual dual-butterfly throttle bodies to two paired units, which narrowed the area required under the airbox and fuel tank. They featured revised—shorter—taper between the secondary throttle valve and the primary. Four-hole injectors replaced single-orifice items for increased fuel flow. The injection system also got a smarter computer, with a 32-bit processor fed by a 22-pole trigger on the crank, replacing an eight-pole unit. This move gave the faster computer more data to work with so it could create finer gradations in the fuel and spark delivery. More accuracy is always better.

They may seem like minor changes, but the big GSX-R gained 10 horsepower at the rear wheel without sacrificing any of the midrange torque that road testers and enthusiasts loved so much about the original GSX-R1000.

Putting that power to the road was an entirely new frame. Since the seminal redesign in 1996, the GSX-R has used a familiar frame technology—cast portions in the steering head and swingarm-pivot area joined by welded sheets of stamped aluminum. For the different models, Suzuki's engineers would specify more or less material thickness in strategic places or call out the addition of stiffeners for the larger bikes. But the overall look and technology were the same.

Starting with the 2003 GSX-R1000, Suzuki made a bold move toward improved technology that promised lower weight and strategically increased stiffness. Where it had used stamped sheets of

BELOW LEFT: Yoshimura Suzuki's 2003 AMA Superbike contender was the new GSX-R1000. Mat Mladin was once again riding behind the 66 number plate after losing the championship to Nicky Hayden in 2002, which was the last year for the Superbike rules that pitted 750cc four-cylinder bikes against 1000cc twins. Now both engine configurations would race at the full liter displacement level.

BELOW RIGHT: Starting the season at Daytona in 2003, Mladin contemplates the new world order aboard 1000cc AMA Superbikes. Despite changing motorcycles over the winter, the Yoshimura team was on the pace immediately, proving not just the diligent application of the team but also the inherent race-bred competence of the bike.

LEFT: The new GSX-R1000 proved to be just as reliable as the familiar 750 and considerably more powerful, as Mladin ably demonstrated as he led the pack at Daytona. In fact, the greatest challenge in the return to 1000cc four-cylinder bikes in AMA Superbike was keeping tires intact.

RIGHT: Kevin Schwantz, working as an advisor to Suzuki, counsels Ben Spies on the tactics needed to win at Daytona.

aluminum, the company turned to extrusions for the main side beams. Modern extrusion technology can make complicated shapes economically and with extremely good consistency.

While recasting the frame, Suzuki's engineers improved the bike's handling by reducing rake by half a degree (from 24.0 to 23.5) and trail by 0.2 inch (3.8 to 3.6). Wheelbase remained the same.

At the same time, the GSX-R1000's suspension components took a major turn toward Superbike tech. Up front, the inverted Showa fork gained a new surface treatment on the sliders called Diamond Like Carbon (DLC). Intended to reduce seal friction (stiction), the DLC treatment was also something of a calling card for the GSX-R and a proud indication of how quickly racing technology could come to the street; the DLC idea was in Superbike racing just a couple of seasons before.

Right next to the DLC stanchions were brakes that represented another bit of racing trickle-down: radial-mount calipers. The idea was simple: by configuring the caliper to mount directly to massive lugs at the bottom of the fork, overall rigidity went up, as did power and braking feel. Increased caliper rigidity also allowed higher brake-line pressures and different pads to be used, all in the search for additional (and predictable) braking power. (A benefit to the race teams was that radial-mount calipers could be used with different-size rotors with the addition of small spacers that did little to compromise overall rigidity.) Because the brakes were more powerful, the discs could be smaller and lighter.

To make the bike feel more compact, the ergonomic profile was changed. The tank was shortened and narrowed slightly, which moved the rider forward and put a bit more weight on the front wheel. This move followed a general movement in motorcycling at the time, as tinier bikes helped shrink the scale of displacement. Today's 750 feels like last year's 600. A middleweight of four years

LEFT: Suzuki continued to do well in the other classes at Daytona. This is Jimmy Moore aboard the GSX-R750 Supersport bike in 2003. **BELOW:** Gregorio Lavilla contested World Superbike for the Alstare team in 2003 and put in several impressive rides on the GSX-R1000. His take-no-prisoners riding style marked him as a classic Suzuki rider.

ABOVE AND RIGHT: What a difference a year makes. After pushing hard to the championship in 2003, Mat Mladin's GSX-R once again wore the number-one plate for the 2004 season, which he would dominate with a bike that continued to develop. Despite Honda's best efforts (and a massive racing budget), the GSX-R would indeed "own the racetrack."

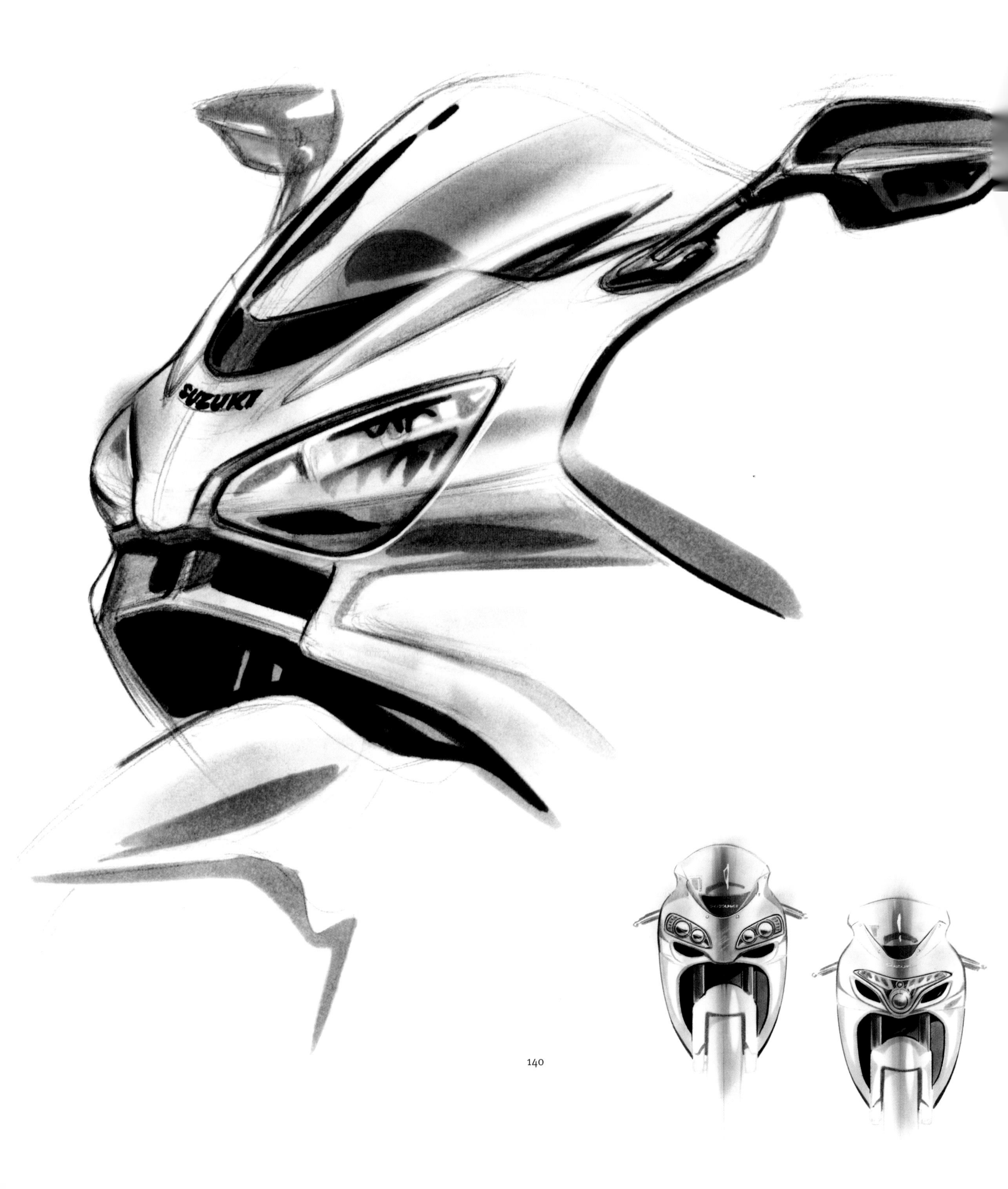
SUZUKI

OPPOSITE: Many iterations of the GSX-R's face were conceived. This set shows an evolution from a more traditional twin-lamp cat eye look with centralized ram-air ducts to a shape more like the final design. Notice, also, the early concept of turn signals in the mirrors, which would actually be used in the 2005 bike. Suzuki's stylists are loath to throw any ideas away.

ago would dwarf a 1000 today. It's a continuation of Mr. Yokouchi's theme set on hyperspeed. Only now horsepower is comparatively easy to come by; the real trick is to keep the bikes along the lighter-is-better trajectory.

In this redesign, Suzuki took a chance on the styling. Whereas before every member of the GSX-R family wore the same clothes, the new 1000 would be noticeably different. (In fact, the previous generation of the 600, 750, and 1000 had slightly different bodywork, but the overall effect was one of close family resemblances, quite deliberately.)

Hiroaki Chosa was the designer who penned the GSX-R1000's detail shape. He's a big fan of fighter aircraft: "I would ride to work right by the Hamamatsu Air Base and see the fighters coming in to land. I loved that look. It's so aggressive and purposeful." Mr. Chosa successfully imbued the GSX-R1000 with those attributes while accepting the challenge of the engineering department, who wanted the ram-air ducts to move closer to the center of the fairing. (The 2001–2002 GSX-R1000's were quite widely spaced by comparison.) "Aerodynamics pushed this part of the design," he acknowledges. "I was given an overall inlet area to work with, but I was free to refine the shape."

ABOVE: The production version of the 2003 GSX-R1000 shows how close the bike came to the concept drawings. A thoughtful use of trim colors helps extend the lines created by the headlight into the upper fairing.

The stacked headlights were intended to recall the Hayabusa, of course, but they share no parts with the GSX1300R. "I wanted a clean and aggressive look," Mr. Chosa says. As for the LED taillights, the shape became a natural extension of the now sharply raked tail section. "But the tail is really just the headlight shape turned upside down," he says.

LEFT: Extensive wind-tunnel development of the GSX-R1000 helped to reduce aerodynamic drag for racing, that's true, but careful attention to detail reduced turbulence for the rider and improved the ram-air system's efficiency for more power at speed. As in Formula 1 car racing, advantages found in the wind tunnel helped bring success on the track.

Suzuki surprised most industry watchers with the immediacy of the updates in only the third year of the bike's life. In comparison tests and on the racetrack, the new GSX-R1000 dominated. Yoshimura and Mladin took another title in AMA Superbike. By every measure, the GSX-R1000 redesign was a smashing success and seemed to put it in a good position to defend the street bike crown as the much-anticipated liter bikes of 2004 were set to debut.

But first, Suzuki stood ready to release two GSX-Rs, a completely new 600 and 750.

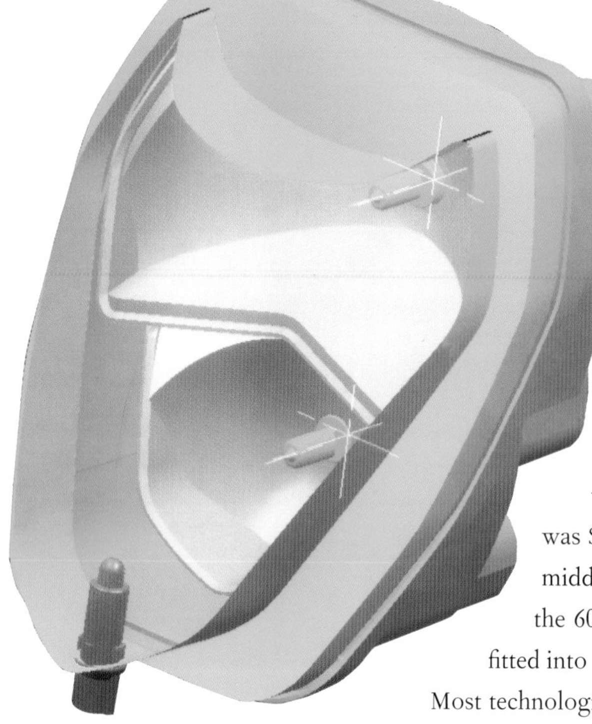

LEFT: Suzuki has long used computer-aided design to back up the styling designer's renderings. This is the computer model of the headlight for the 1000. Such modeling can help determine the final shape of the lens for optimum light dispersion. Knowing the precise shape of the back of the lens also helps the instrument-panel engineers integrate their work.
RIGHT: The GSX-R1000's LED taillight array proved to be lighter and more energy efficient than conventional incandescent bulbs. What's more, its shape was defined by the headlight's and simply inverted.

Again, the company turned its engineering trends ninety degrees from what was expected. Before, all the 600s were based on the 750s—same size, based on the same engine cases, and so on. This time around, seeing that the 600 class only continued to grow and that the 750 class was Suzuki's for the taking, the emphasis turned instead to the middleweight. As a result, the 750—unquestionably more like the 600 than ever—became extremely compact, just as the 600 fitted into the (small) box of a 600cc Supersport.

Most technologies applied to the 2003 GSX-R1000 were visited upon the 2004 GSX-R600 and 750. New extruded-section main frame. Check. Radial-mount front brake calipers. Check. More aggressive, angular styling. Check. More power. Yes, indeed.

Although the bottom ends of both engines remained true to their predecessors, both bikes got new heads and the paired throttle bodies first seen on the 1000. (The other injection upgrades, from a faster processor to a more accurate timing sensor, were applied here as well.)

The 600 received a new cylinder head of familiar architecture. The included valve angle was reduced to a thoroughly modern 22 degrees (from 28), allowing the intake ports to become straighter and more efficient. New pistons with flat tops worked with the smaller combustion chambers for a higher, 12.5:1 compression ratio. And—the ultimate treat of technophiles—the sixteen valves were now constructed of superlight titanium. Yes, a production motorcycle—good for thousands of miles on the street and carrying a full warranty plus a competitive price tag—now had titanium valves. Suzuki turned to them for extra durability at elevated revs, but that's not all. Lighter valves can handle more aggressive cam timing, and they do so with lighter springs. As you'd expect, the new 600's (and 750's) springs were lighter than the previous versions, which helped reduce frictional losses in the engine. The upper piston rings were faced with a chrome-nitride plating to reduce friction. Crank main journals were reduced in width by 2mm. Once more, Suzuki had gone back to the precepts that built the first GSX-R: keep looking for improvements even in the smallest increments.

BELOW: Even such seemingly plain details as the fuel cap are well considered by the styling designers. Here are three proposals for the new 1000, each a subtly different variation on the theme.

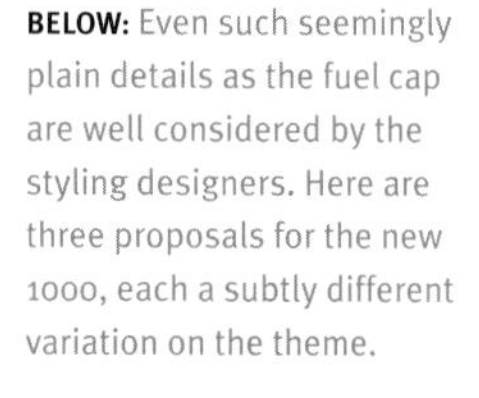

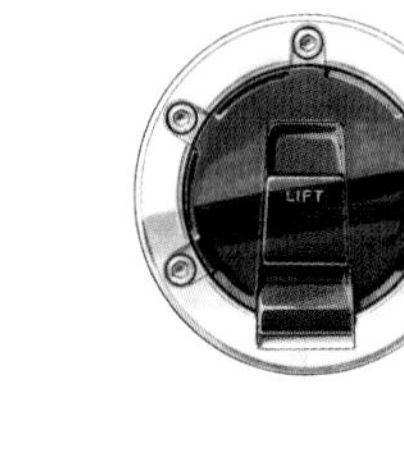

In general specification, the '04 GSX-R600's engine wasn't very far down the development chain from the '03 bike's, but it made more power at higher rpm and was lighter, thanks in part to a comprehensive weight-reduction program that pared weight from the high-strength cast-iron camshafts to the cylinder hold-down bolts.

BELOW: Four-color renderings of the GSX-R1000 show how subtle changes of color and striping can have a big impact on the overall appearance. At Suzuki, many of the styling designers will rotate into a supporting role as color designers for other designers' bodywork creations.

LEFT: Early proposals for a new instrument cluster ranged from simple to extravagant. For all, the tach was the central feature, with ancillary readouts committed to LCD screens. The final version incorporated a shift light and large LCD numerals for improved legibility. **BELOW:** These caliper mock-ups show the extent to which modern styling influences design. Look closely and you'll notice that each is slightly different. The version chosen is at the top.

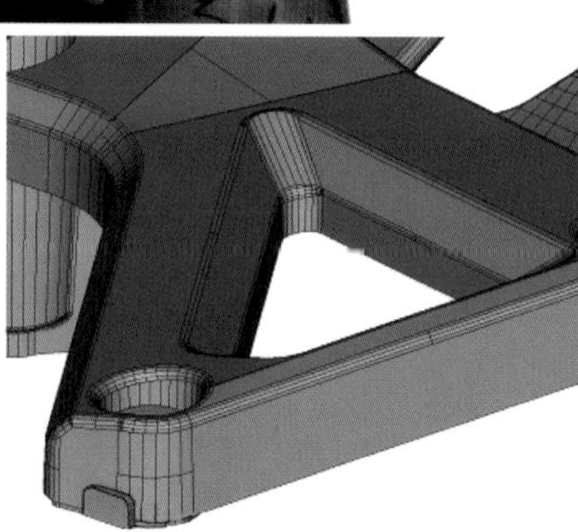

TOP: This is an example of how no styling option is left unexamined. Suzuki considered many taillight designs during the development of the 2004 GSX-R600 and 750. Some closely followed the pattern set by the 2003 GSX-R1000; others significantly diverged from any family resemblance. **ABOVE RIGHT:** Suzuki employs a great deal of computer-aided design (CAD) in the development of the GSX-R line. Here, details of the cast-aluminum subframe are shown. CAD can help determine load requirements as well as create a virtual motorcycle to see how each component fits with the others. **ABOVE LEFT:** The now-trademark large ram-air scoops dominate this styling exercise, but the split headlamps were not, obviously, chosen for production.

In fact, every part on the new 600 and 750 was scrutinized for flab. The aluminum radiator was lighter than before but more efficient. The engine control unit was smaller and lighter yet more powerful.

Dimensionally, both the 600 and 750 were quite a bit tidier than their predecessors. For the 600, the wheelbase was left alone (it was already shorter than the 750's), rake tucked in by 0.75 degree (to a very race bike-like 23.25 degrees), and trail diminished to 3.7 inches from 3.8. The 750 got a wheelbase reduction of 0.4 inch to 55.1, the same as the 600. Rake came in to 23.6 degrees with the same 3.7 inches of trail as the 600.

From the rider's perspective, both bikes became perceptibly smaller. The new fuel injection system allowed the throttle bodies to be pulled together and the airbox to be smaller, which in turn allowed the tank to be smaller than before. It tapped in at 0.6 inch (15mm) shorter and 1.2 inch (30mm) narrower at the knee-grip point than before. Seat height dropped by a useful 0.2 inch (5mm).

By tradition, the 600 and 750 kept suspension components from Showa, with the only difference between them the set up specification. This change brought the 600 to the world of inverted fork legs (again) and gave both bikes the coveted radial-mount front brake calipers. But the new bikes went their big brother one better with a radial master cylinder, which is pure race stuff intended to improve power and bump feedback. As much as possible, the 600 and 750 were exactly alike. That extended even to the new, braced swingarm; historically, the 600 received a simple, nonbraced unit and the 750 got the trick stuff. Now it was the same piece for both bikes.

With the new rapid product cycles in place, it wasn't possible to keep the same designer on the GSX-R line. This was quite a change from the days when Mr. Ishii presided over two and a half generations of GSX-Rs, spanning seven model years.

Hidezumi Kato, the 2004 bike's designer, was another young gun with a sharp sense of style. His objectives in the new 600 and 750 were to take the 2003 GSX-R1000 as the starting point but not be tied down by it. As ever, aerodynamic requirements set a limit on raw possibilities. "I needed to re-

ABOVE: These design studies (the two on the left) looked into maintaining a tall fuel tank whose lower edge came right down to the frame rails. Careful use of character lines in the upper surfaces of the tank mitigate the visual height of such an arrangement. Initial profile mock-ups (the two images on the right) show the various styling directions considered. Notice the difference in tank height and the large void under the tank to reveal the engine compartment.

BELOW: For the 2003 GSX-R1000, Suzuki developed new diamond-spoke wheels that were lighter than the previous round-spoke hoops yet stronger. Reducing unsprung weight not only improved acceleration but also helped make the bike considerably more agile and responsive. Suzuki wanted the revised 1000 to feel much more like the 750 than before.

RIGHT: With the design finalized, the GSX-R's headlight goes into production engineering, where its shape and substance will be defined by the computer. The 2004 600 and 750 received a special combination of projector-style low beam and multireflector high beam.

BELOW LEFT AND RIGHT: These two headlight mock-ups may look very much alike, but the simple matter of changing the overall height of the headlight has a big impact on the styling. Here, a smaller headlight was simulated (by computer) next to the assembly that was eventually put into production.

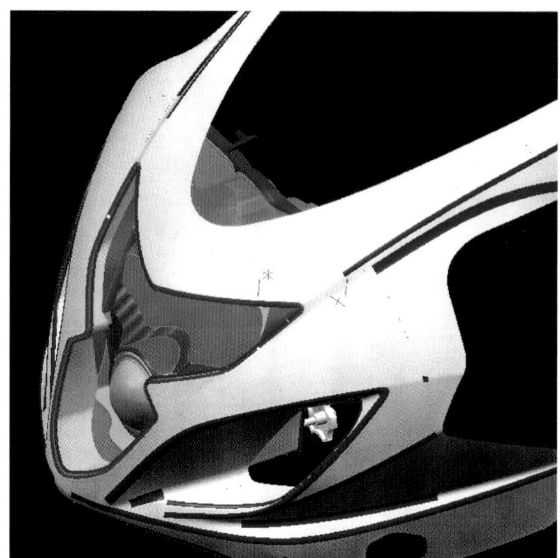

tain the narrow face and close-set ram-air intakes," he says. "But I was free to work on many surfaces, including the forward fairing. I wanted the bike to look good when on the track, so there are no bumps or posts for the mirrors. When they come off, the surface is flat and smooth." He also worked with the aerodynamicists to fine-tune the bike's profile. "These," he says, pointing to the triangular flicks on the trailing edge of the front fairing, "are to smooth the airflow. They had to be this shape to maintain clearance for the rider's hands."

Mr. Kato also worked hard to minimize the bike's visual mass. For example, the fuel tank had black panels bordering the frame. Not only did this reduce the visual height of the tank, but it helped hide a large portion of the seam. The forward strake of the rear bodywork was angled perfectly to pick up this character line started in the tank. Another character line on the top of the tank—most visible when you're sitting on the bike—also reduced visual height while preserving room for sufficient fuel and an efficient airbox.

Considering the limitations placed on the designer by the engineering department—the current design mantra remained as it was in the beginning, performance before anything else—the new crop of talent was extremely successful in keeping the GSX-R's styling modern.

As model year 2004 wound down, little would anyone appreciate that Suzuki's newfound sense of style and adventurousness was just starting to emerge. In response to dramatically elevated opposition in the open class—"We were, honestly, a bit surprised by the competition in 2004," says Mr. Iguchi—Suzuki was preparing an entirely new GSX-R1000 that would ring in the model's twentieth anniversary by, once more, thoroughly thrashing its rivals.

20th Anniversary GSX-R600 and 750

For 2005, Suzuki released a limited run of 20th Anniversary 600s and 750s. The regular models were unchanged from 2004 specifications. The 600 and 750 were marked by cosmetic distinctions. A special blue paint scheme and blue seat recalled the lighter hue of the first-generation GSX-R750. The chain had blue-anodized side plates, and frame sliders were standard. The muffler had a black wrap instead of the spun silver of the regular bike. Special slotted brake discs with higher radiation efficiency were standard. The only mechanical change of note is that the 600 received the 750's larger, trapezoidal radiator—no doubt a nod to Supersport racing demands.

LEFT: To further distinguish the 20th Anniversary models from the regular production run of 2005 GSX-R600s and 750s, the chain carried distinctive blue-anodized side plates. **BELOW:** As a special celebration of the GSX-R's twentieth anniversary, Suzuki built a limited number of specially outfitted GSX-R600s and 750s. Mechanically, they were almost identical to the standard versions—with the primary difference being the 600's use of the 750's radiator—but they had distinctive paint schemes in colors that paid homage to the original race-bike-with-lights GSX-R.

ABOVE LEFT: Special 20th Anniversary models received a numbered plate on the upper triple clamp. **ABOVE RIGHT:** The 20th Anniversary edition of the GSX-R600 gained the 750's larger, trapezoidal radiator for improved cooling—despite the fact that in street guise the 600 was sufficiently cooled. However, competition places increased strain on the engine and cooling system. Racing, again, informed the design. **RIGHT:** Special slotted brake discs on the twentieth anniversary models were designed to improve heat dissipation and braking feel. The four-piston radial-mount calipers were the same as those on the standard edition 600 and 750.

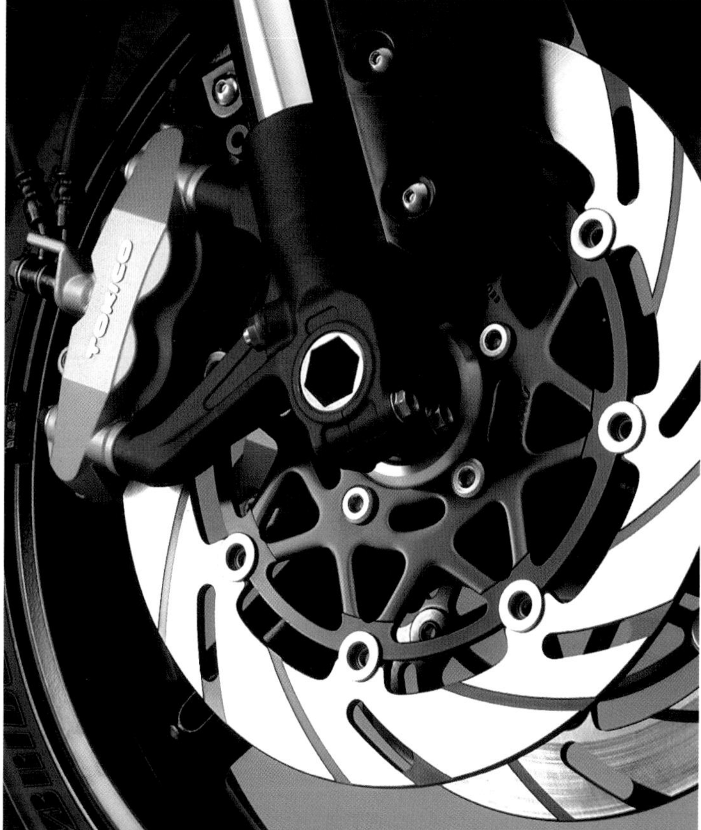

CHAPTER 8

THE NEW GSX-R1000 CULMINATES TWO DECADES OF GSX-R DEVELOPMENT

Generation 7: 2005 On

OPPOSITE: An early design sketch shows the GSX-R1000's subtle shift away from the styling paradigms of the 2004 GSX-R600 and 750. The textured, multi-layered side fairings evident in this image suggest that such surface treatment was a high priority even before the model was far along in its gestation.

BELOW: Aaron Yates contested 1000cc Superstock and Superbike for Team Yoshimura in 2005, joining five-time champion Mat Mladin and up-and-comer Ben Spies on the 2005 GSX-R1000.

The 2005 GSX-R1000—Suzuki's unquestioned flagship and the best birthday present imaginable for the GSX-R line—is more than what it appears to be. It is not just another step along the inexorable evolution of the brand but the first product of what is a fundamental shift in the way Suzuki designs motorcycles.

First, though, an explanation. With the possible exception of the first liquid-cooled models, the push in GSX-R development has come from the engineering and racing departments. What will make it a better sportbike? What will make it a better race bike? Where has the competition started to catch up? Where are we ahead? How can we bring high technology into production at a reasonable cost?

All these questions and their answers came from the ranks of engineers who sought to quantify what is a great motorcycle and, in doing so, allowed themselves an avenue to improve it. Could it be made lighter? Smaller? More powerful? These attributes are easily put into a spreadsheet or proven on a scale or dynamometer.

As a result of this engineering-is-all focus, the stylists often got to the bike so far along in the process that their options were limited. Moreover, the overarching philosophy of keeping the GSX-R close to race theology has, historically, pushed for conservative styling. After all, race bikes are purely about function and performance; their beauty comes from the performance as much as (and often more than) from the design.

It comes to this: with the new GSX-R, the stylists

ABOVE: Experienced hands at the Yoshimura Suzuki factory team—Don Sakakura (center) and Kevin Schwantz (right)—help young gun Ben Spies hone his considerable talent into winning racecraft. In May 2005, Spies broke through to win his first AMA Superbike race at Fontana in California, holding off a determined charge by 2003 World Superbike champion Neil Hodgson.

BELOW: Andrew Trevitt from *Sport Rider* magazine attended the launch at the Phillip Island circuit in Australia. He says, "My notes from the GSX-R's press launch pretty much sum things up: After the second session, I opened my pad, sat looking at a blank sheet for about 10 minutes, and wrote 'There's really nothing wrong with this bike.' It's easily more motorcycle than 90 percent of its buyers will know what to do with."

have had a freer hand. Shuji Matsuzawa—wiry, young, and slightly introverted—is the architect of the latest GSX-R's stunning curves. "I wanted something very dynamic but distinctive. The GSX-Rs all have a family face, but this one had to have more emotion," he says. Emotion. That's not something the engineering staff would readily paste onto the list of development goals.

"The side panels are three-dimensional," continues Mr. Matsuzawa. "We were able to produce these parts to a very high finish and give the side of the bike more emotion." There it is again: emotion. These fairing pieces are actually separate items, replacing the slab-sided construction that debuted with the first GSX-R.

Plenty of changes took place during the development of the new GSX-R. "The original headlight design was curved straight across, from tip to tip," says Mr. Matsuzawa. "But the test riders said the illumination needed to be better, so we added the upward arch in the center." The headlight retains the stacked configuration but with two conventional bulbs and multifaceted reflectors. (This deviation from the 600 and 750 style, which used a projector-beam main unit, was to further distance the 1000 from its smaller brethren.)

Racing, as ever, drove the design of the GSX-R's bodywork. "After wind-tunnel work, it was decided to reduce the width of the fairing and bring the ram-air ducts closer to the center," says Mr. Matsuzawa. "Also, we changed the shape of the lower fairing in front of the rear tire so that it would receive better cooling. That was a request of the racing department." Overall, the new GSX-R is 5 percent cleaner, aerodynamically.

ABOVE LEFT: Mat Mladin and Team Yoshimura Suzuki have been a match made for the record books. A finely tuned crew working with a motivated and undeniably talented rider have helped take an already competitive motorcycle to the pinnacle of the class. **BELOW LEFT:** Domination from the very start: Mat Mladin starts on pole for the Daytona Superbike race and would go on to stamp the event as his own. More important to Suzuki, the Yoshimura team kept the rest of the field at bay, including the once-powerful Hondas. (Honda would later refer to 2005 as a "development season," despite the fact that the 2005 GSX-R1000 was truly an all-new bike competing against the CBR1000RR, which had a year's development already.)

TOP: Troy Corser joined Yukio Kagayama on the podium in Qatar at the first World Superbike race of the 2005 season. (Alongside is Ducati's Regis Laconi.) Not only did the GSX-R1000 win the first time out in 2005, the team won the first seven of eight races in the World Superbike calendar, with Corser taking six to Kagayama's one. It was an impressive start to the season. **ABOVE LEFT:** Troy Corser's World Superbike GSX-R1000 is a well-developed race bike that benefited from the extensive testing and race experience of both the AMA Superbike and the World Superbike teams throughout 2003 and 2004. It came off the trailer, as they say, very much on the pace. Its progressive—yet still stunning—power delivery made the best use of the spec Pirelli tires in the 2005 season. **ABOVE RIGHT:** Masayuki Itoh is a familiar face to ardent race watchers even if they don't know his name. He forms the critical link between Yoshimura Suzuki and the factory, and he is responsible for the close interaction of the Yoshimura team and the factory engineers not just because he is widely respected in Hamamatsu, but also because this method has been remarkably successful for both parties over the years.

DUNLOP
AIR LIFT

Other notable aspects of the design were conceived to simplify the look and better integrate the necessary evils of street-going motorcycles—lights, mirrors, and turn signals. Placing the front turn signals in the mirrors is not a huge leap of faith in styling, but, as Mr. Matsuzawa says, "It was done so that when you take [the GSX-R] to the track, you won't have to remove the signals." In other words, take off the mirrors, and the signals go along for the ride.

Freedoms were found elsewhere. "I was free to style the top of the seat cowl and reproduced a character element from the tank," says Mr. Matsuzawa. "As long as the seat cowl was a certain height from the seat—set by aerodynamic needs—I could do what I wanted there." Suzuki's tests showed increased stability at high speed when the top of the seat cowl was a certain shape and height. In particular, it had to slope down from the rider's back, not form a sharp angle when viewed in profile. This, more than anything else, explains why most modern sportbikes have similar-appearing seat cowls. Once more, function wins.

At Suzuki, the 2005 GSX-R1000 represents a shift toward more freedom for the designers, that's true, but it also inaugurates a new, more efficient way of developing motorcycles. As the company was bringing the 2005 GSX-R1000 to life, plans were already in place to move the research and development teams from the company headquarters in Hamamatsu to the testing facility at Ryuyo. Merging operations at Ryuyo has the benefit of closing the loop between development and test riding. In fact, placing virtually all motorcycle development in one place will help accelerate the process of introducing new models into the white-hot Superbike market segment. "It is now necessary to keep the GSX-R on a [tight] product cycle," says Hiroshi Iio, current chief engineer for the motorcycle group and the man responsible for the latest GSX-R1000. "Our competitors are moving rapidly, and we need to work hard to stay ahead of them. If you stand still, you fall behind."

A significant part of the development centered on the GSX-R's engine. It is based on the previous design, but nonetheless thoroughly updated. Extra displacement—from 988cc to 999cc—comes entirely through a larger bore. This is, in one sense, not a surprise, as the previous engine's 59mm stroke was the longest in the class. For 2005, it remains so. But increasing bore size on an engine that retains its 80mm bore spacing—the same as the 750 introduced in '96—requires extremely high-tech materials. The engine retains SCEM linerless construction—a nickel-phosphorous-silicon-carbide antiwear surface is applied to the base aluminum bores—that keeps the cylinder block compact and helps promote fast, efficient heat transfer.

OPPOSITE: Team Yoshimura's immaculate, efficient shop in Southern California prepares all the bikes for the AMA Superbike, Supersport, and Superstock series. The team enjoys a tight and symbiotic relationship with the Suzuki factory. Team manager Don Sakakura says, "A lot of what we do here [modifying bikes for racing] ends up in the production models."

BELOW: Preproduction renderings of the 2005 GSX-R1000's nose explored various styling options. Notice that this image is very close to the 2004 GSX-R750, including the projector low-beam assembly that was not used on the production 2005 GSX-R1000.

OPPOSITE: This styling exercise is considerably further along. Notice how the decision to run turn signals in the mirrors had already been made, but the headlight had yet to be finalized.

BELOW: In 2005, Hiroshi Iio was the chief engineer for the motorcycle group and the man responsible for the latest GSX-R1000. "Our competitors are moving rapidly, and we need to work hard to stay ahead of them," he says. "If you stand still, you fall behind."

Although the bottom end is largely the same, small adjustments to the cylinder head increase efficiency as well. The shape is subtly changed and, along with the larger bore, results in a higher compression ratio, up to 12.5:1 from 12.0:1 in the 2004 bike. Like the 600 and 750 in 2004, the new 1000 gets titanium valves; they are lighter than the steel valves they replace by 5.4 grams each (intake) and 6.4 grams (exhaust). The intake valves are 1mm larger in diameter, and all valves have flat bottoms instead of radiused faces. Lighter valves allow for lighter springs, which in turn allow for a safely raised redline, up to 13,500 rpm.

Riding in those larger bores are new pistons that are 8 grams lighter each. They carry three rings each. As on the 600 and 750, the oil-control ring has a special low-friction face, and the top compression ring is L-shaped for reduced weight. In all, the piston pack is lighter and lower friction than before.

To keep this high-compression engine cool, the GSX-R1000 has a new radiator that's slightly thinner but a bit wider and taller than before; it has 13 percent more cooling capacity. It's so good that the Yoshimura AMA Superbike team uses the production radiator without modification. "It's very efficient. We use the stock part right off the production bike," says Yoshimura team manager Don Sakakura.

Changes to the largest GSX-R's intake and exhaust systems also help keep the competition at bay. A new dual-injector system retains the dual-throttle-valve technology that debuted with the 2000 GSX-R750, albeit in a highly evolved state. The primary injector is where the sole injector is

OPPOSITE: This is a relatively late styling illustration, as evidenced by the side fairing's resemblance to the actual production item. Styling designers are constantly fine-tuning the design as it nears production.

BELOW: Again, racing necessity helps provide a link back to the street bike. Suzuki's MotoGP contender, the GSV-R, carries significant styling links from the GSX-R1000. Or is it the other way around?

on the 2004 machine, facing the primary throttle butterfly and angled so that at full throttle the fuel stream strikes the plate for better atomization. The secondary injector is upstream but still below the secondary throttle—many other dual-injection systems place the second injector above the throttle body in the inlet trumpet. Suzuki's system is more compact and efficient.

On the other side of the engine is what may be the GSX-R1000's most distinctive technology: a fully titanium exhaust system with a short, highly tapered muffler. Suzuki's engineers admit to trying an underseat—or "center-up"—exhaust system but rejected it on several points. "It was heavier than the system we have now," explains Mr. Iio. "And it hurt the handling of the bike. We wanted to keep the bike's mass centralized, but the heavy center-up system moved weight back and up." Put another way, it didn't work as well as the tried-and-true low system, so it was scrapped. This decision should not be taken any other way than this: Suzuki considered alternatives, but for the GSX-R and its extremely well-defined mission, they simply weren't as good. Performance comes before following fashion. End of story.

Instead, the exhaust system, which retains the torque-enhancing SET valve, was shaped to maximize cornering clearance and to move mass close to the center of the bike. That's one reason it's shorter than the more traditional muffler worn by the 2004 bike.

Altogether, the GSX-R1000's engine changes—subtle though they may seem—brought an extra 14 hp with no loss of midrange torque.

Matsuzawa

Matsuzawa

They say power is nothing without control, and that's partly why the GSX-R1000 received a new race-style slipper clutch for 2005. A special cam mechanism in the clutch assembly allows it to slip a set amount during aggressive downshifts, which in turn helps reduce rear-wheel lockup under racing conditions. "This is another way racing experience has improved the street bike," says Hironori Iguchi, director of motorcycle engineering.

Incremental improvements were applied throughout the new 1000's chassis as well. Larger-diameter front brake rotors (up to 310mm from 300mm) allied with a radial master cylinder promise improved brake performance.

Chassis geometry was juggled yet again, with the aim of improved steering response and agility while retaining stability. (As bikes get lighter and faster, it becomes ever harder to achieve the ideal balance, which is why every manufacturer seems to be shifting geometry year to year, a tenth of a degree here, a few millimeters of trail there ... it's all to hone handling to a sharp, shiny edge.) For the 2005 GSX-R1000, rake was let out slightly (23.8 degrees vs. 23.5), trail was increased (3.8 inches, up from 3.6), yet the wheelbase was reduced slightly (55.3 inches, down from 55.5). Overall length, height, and width were also reduced slightly; in total, the new 1000 is more compact, smaller even than many middleweight sportbikes.

Riders will look at the spec sheet and wonder if perhaps it isn't underestimating the shrinkage. That's because the ergonomic profile has changed massively. The seat is 0.8 inch (20mm) lower, while the distance from the seat to the handlebars has shrunk 1.6 inches (40mm). These changes are the result of a shorter tank—thanks in part to the smaller airbox under the svelte fuel tank—and a shrink-wrapped frame. The frame is 0.2 inch shorter from the steering head to the swingarm pivot. From a materials point of view it has morphed as well. The cast steering-head assembly is longer than on the 2004 bike, and the extruded side beams incorporate a different reinforcing rib. The rear subframe has been changed from a combination of cast and extruded members to a two-piece casting with a removable rear section—better for racing. The total frame is nearly 5 pounds lighter, with its stiffness improved for better feedback.

ABOVE: Design drawings for the GSX-R1000 reveal exploration of various shapes and surfaces. Although there were many iterations that tried differing styles of exhaust, by the time these were being developed, the final-design muffler had already been decided upon.

OPPOSITE: Initial styling concepts show where the radical form of the production GSX-R1000 came from. Suzuki's styling designers were asked to take this model to a higher level of styling and overall design.

LEFT: The shape of the ram-air ducts is critical to maintaining maximum pressure recovery.
BELOW: For the GSX-R1000, a new styling tack involved placing the turn signals in the mirrors, which helps clean up the shape of the lower fairing and provides the 1000 with a distinctly sleek appearance.

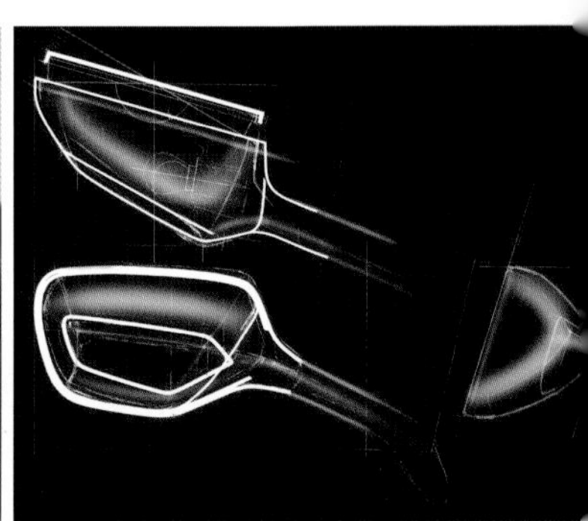

ABOVE: Suzuki considered several variations on the new instrument cluster, including a stacked layout and one with an LCD bar graph tachometer. The final item (the third in the row) includes a gear-position indicator and low-fuel trip-meter that starts counting miles after the low-fuel light comes on. **RIGHT:** One proposed instrument cluster treatment is virtually mocked-up in the cockpit to help determine how the piece would look in place and to get a first indication of legibility.

LEFT: Suzuki spent a considerable amount of time in the wind tunnel with the GSX-R1000. The intent was to improve its overall drag coefficient, but just as important was the effort to shape the bike so that it would be stable at speed. Various detail refinements, including the way the top of the seat cowl picks up air coming off the rider's back, help improve aerodynamics.

Similarly, the new swingarm uses a combination of cast and extruded pieces, and it is designed for selective flexibility for improved control while the bike is cornering. The right side is specially tucked in to make room for the exhaust system.

Because, as Mr. Yokouchi maintained from the first glimmer of the GSX-R750's development, weight is the enemy, the new 1000 was worked over from stem to stern in the search for do-nothing weight. The frame accounted for 2.4 pounds; the wheels, a pound; the engine, half a pound (even the cylinder-head bolts went on a diet); the battery, a pound. In the end, the new GSX-R steps into a new open-class power play at 366 pounds dry. That's 4 less than the 2003 bike and 9 under the original 2001 GSX-R1000.

The early press reports from the GSX-R1000's launch at Phillip Island, Australia, were glowing. From *Motorcyclist*, Tim Carrithers says: "After looking at pictures of the thing for the last six months, two things are clear. It's better looking in person, and it's small. Imagine an angular, ⅞-sized translation of the '04 bike. In every salient dimension but horsepower, there's less to it this year than last. Armed with the sort of power delivery you'd expect from an Ohio-class nuclear submarine, there's enough thrust to cruise around the track without leaving the relative comfort of fourth gear."

Cycle World's Don Canet reported from Australia, "The first thing you notice when settling into the '05's saddle is that the bike is significantly more compact than before." Of the new engine's character, he says, "Broad and linear best describes the torque spread of the new GSX-R mill." And, summing up, he continues, "I have no doubt that the Suzuki has the Kawi [ZX-10R] covered

OPPOSITE: While the GSX-R1000 was developed with a strong emphasis on racetrack performance, Suzuki's engineers never forgot that it would be, first and foremost, a street bike. As a result, the GSX-R's roadgoing manners received a tremendous amount of attention—no small order when the power-to-weight ratio is as impressive as the 1000's is.

LEFT: Scraping clay off the model in the wind tunnel, a Suzuki technician makes subtle changes to see how they affect the aerodynamic profile of the bike.

RIGHT: Shuji Matsuzawa was the styling designer on the GSX-R1000. "I wanted something very dynamic but distinctive," he says.

in terms of handling composure, even when banging down through the gears into a slow corner. At these elevated performance levels, composure is key in breeding confidence that's tough to beat."

Around the same time the journalists got their first taste of the new GSX-R1000, its mettle was proven on the racetrack. It won the first two races in the 2005 World Superbike calendar, at Qatar. Riders Troy Corser and Yukio Kagayama made it look easy, with Corser four seconds in the lead when rain shortened the second race. After promising performances with the previous-generation GSX-R1000 in WSB, the 2005 model's dominant performance in its first two races was a genuine breakthrough.

On American soil, Yoshimura Suzuki rider and five-time AMA Superbike champion Mat Mladin dominated the Daytona event, shortened to a sprint race from its traditional 200-mile format. Though quick to credit the team for his success, Mladin says, "Both the Yoshimura Suzuki GSX-R750 and GSX-R1000 motorbikes were and still are very competitive. We have had great success on both bikes. We won three AMA Superbike titles on the 750, and so far, we've won two on the 1000." The unspoken belief is that number six will come if the early form holds.

As much as Suzuki loves to win championships in pure racing forms, it was ecstatic to win the first Superstock race of 2005 with rider Vincent Haskovec. Aboard the Team M4 EMGO Suzuki, he managed to beat Team Yoshimura rider Aaron Yates and Jordan Motorsports rider Jason Pridmore for a Suzuki takeover of the podium. Second-place finisher Yates said, "It's a long championship, and it's great that Suzuki swept the podium. The GSX-R1000 is definitely the best bike out there." For Suzuki's engineering staff, this result was incredibly satisfying as it proved the performance of the bike in near-stock form and, once again, validated the concept of transferring race experience and know-how to the production models. Not only did the extensive engineering changes that

SUZUKI
Arai

BELOW: This view with the bodywork off shows just how densely packed the GSX-R1000's chassis really is. The engine—indeed all the heaviest components—have been moved toward the center of the bike to reduce polar moments and improve handling.

brought the new GSX-1000 make it a better street bike, its early performance in 2005 proved it a great race bike, right out of the crate.

Yoshimura Suzuki rider Ben Spies finished fourth in the Superbike race at Daytona and fourth in the 600cc Supersport race. He moved up to the Superbike squad for 2005 after three years in the AMA Supersport, Formula Extreme, and Superstock classes; he was the 2003 Formula Extreme champion. "I can't imagine a better bike to make my Superbike debut on than the Yoshimura Suzuki GSX-R1000," he says. "The bike makes me feel comfortable and fast and almost invincible. The level of development from Suzuki is amazing. The engineers in Japan don't just stop at some given time. They are constantly coming here to the U.S. and acting as a support base at our tests and races. They listen to everything we have to say and really pay attention. My crew is welcome to ask tech support questions day or night on the Internet. I can't say enough about Suzuki Japan or American Suzuki."

To fully appreciate the relentless march of technology and the hard work of Suzuki's engineers, you need to remember this: the original GSX-R750, a gobsmacking revolution in weight and power, the undisputed lightweight of sporting motorcycles, was, despite dropping jaws all over motorcycling, nearly 30 pounds heavier.

And, with 80 rear-wheel horsepower, almost exactly half as powerful.

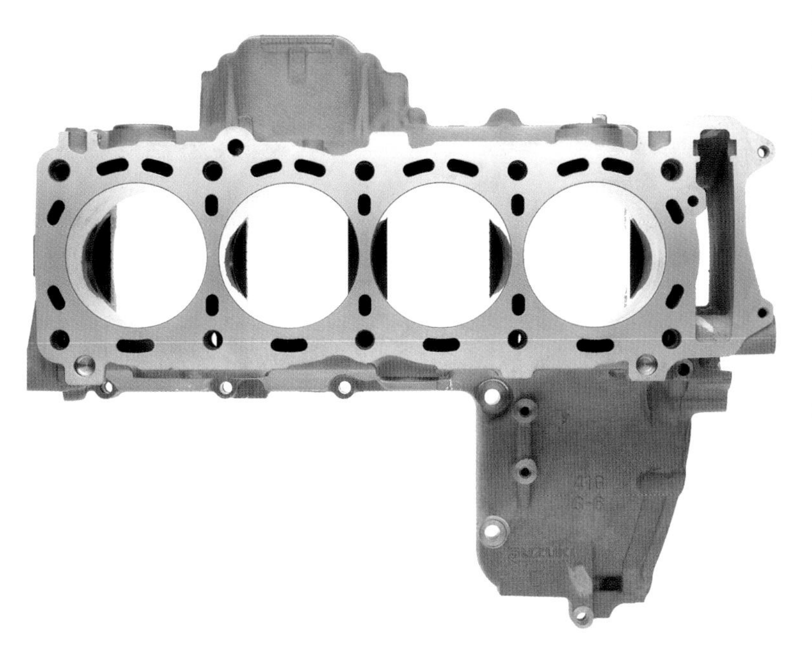

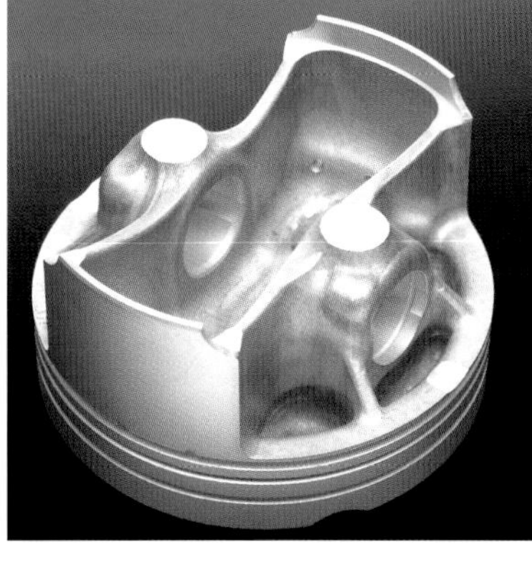

ABOVE LEFT: For the GSX-R1000, Suzuki developed a back-torque-limiting clutch. This race-proven technology permits the rider to make quick downshifts in succession without worrying about locking up the rear wheel with engine braking. **BELOW LEFT:** The GSX-R1000's new pistons are lighter, despite being 0.4mm wider, than those used in the 2004's engine. Lowered reciprocating weight improves engine responsiveness and allows a higher redline for improved top-end power. **FAR LEFT:** Subtly modified, the GSX-R1000's cylinder block features a closed-deck design for maximum rigidity and extremely tight bore spacing to keep the engine narrow. Suzuki's distinctive SCEM composite metallic coating covers the bores.

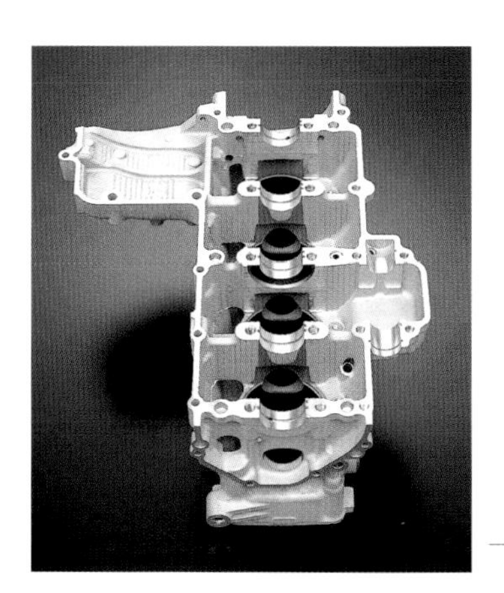

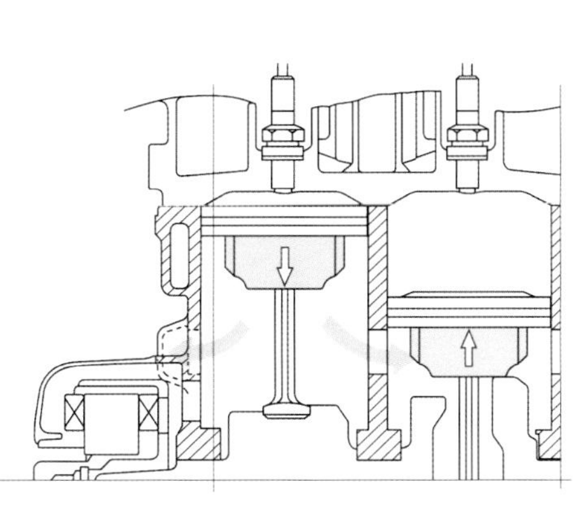

ABOVE: To improve overall efficiency, Suzuki placed ports in the crankcase above the bearing webs to allow pressure under the pistons to equalize. In this way, the descending piston meets little or no air resistance, which prevents the loss of horsepower and efficiency that occurs in conventional engines. **RIGHT:** From the outside, the GSX-R1000's engine appears much like the previous bike's, but myriad internal changes and a slight increase in displacement yield a 14 percent increase in power.

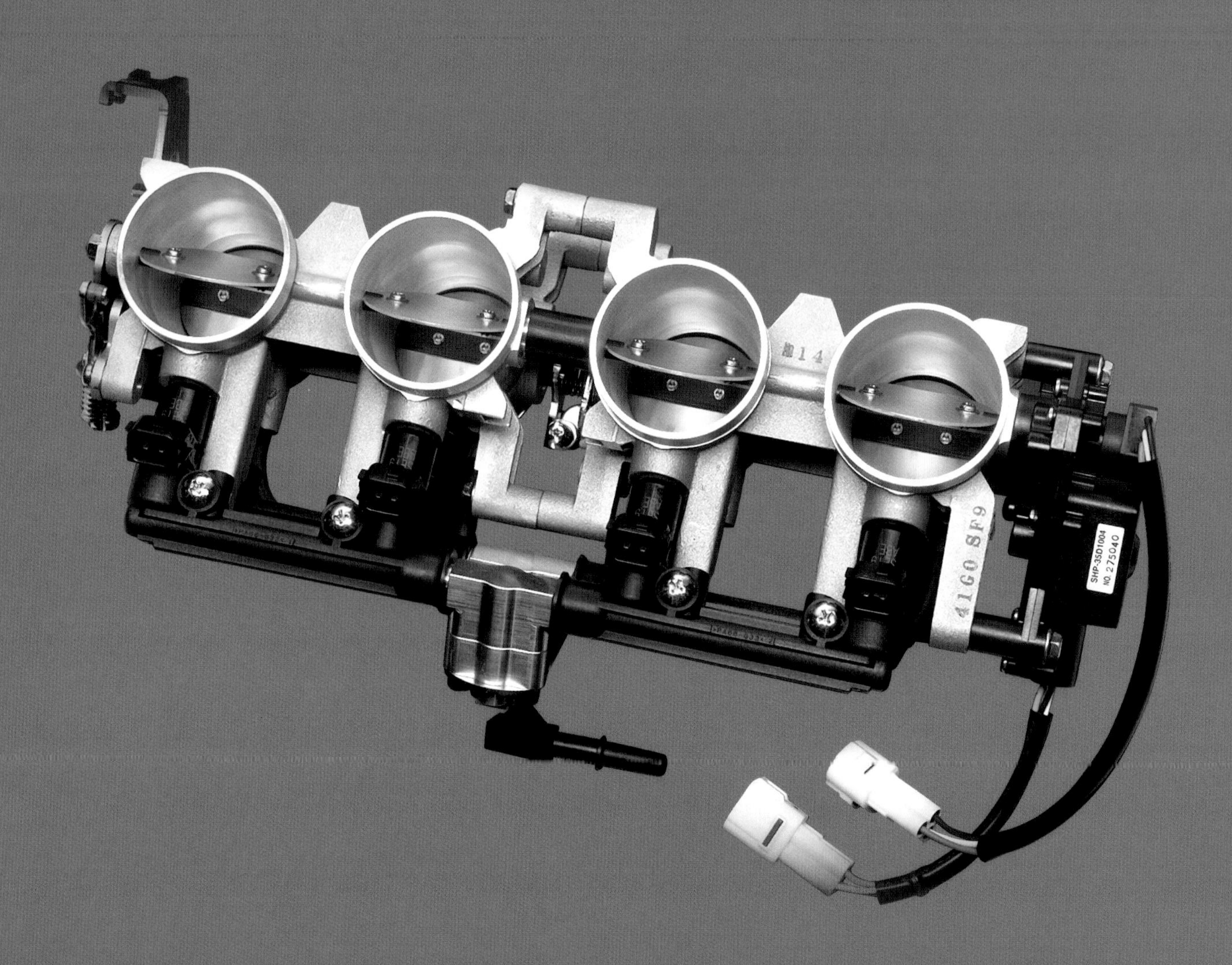

ABOVE AND RIGHT: An entirely new adaptation of Suzuki's distinctive SDTV dual-throttle-valve fuel injection was used on the 2005 GSX-R1000. The greatest change was a move to dual fuel injectors, which help improve maximum power output while retaining excellent throttle response. The angles of the injectors in the throttle body were carefully chosen to improve fuel atomization.

Development at Suzuki

Refinement of the next generation of GSX-Rs will, surely, be at a breakneck pace, but it will nevertheless follow essentially the same path as that of the new 1000. The hierarchy seems confusing but is actually straightforward. A project leader is assigned to the bike and then works with product planning to figure out where the bike needs to go in terms of development. Then there are heads of engine and chassis engineering for the project, as well as styling designers and color designers.

After initial concepting, which takes place between the project leader and engineering, the chassis and engine teams work independently on their specific tasks. Their goals are easily imagined: less weight, more power, better handling. They are, however, kept connected through the management levels in engineering so that the solutions are closely meshed. A slight improvement in one place—say, a reduction in cylinder height—is immediately capitalized upon by the chassis engineers.

During this phase, the motorcycle begins to literally take shape. Depending upon the changes envisioned, a new chassis may be tested with the existing engine or a new engine design may be fitted temporarily to the current chassis. This happens well after the engine has seen many hours on the dyno, of course, or after the chassis has been through a preliminary review. These prototype mules are carefully camouflaged, but the fact that Suzuki can carry out much of its development in private at Ryuyo helps tremendously.

Many tasks take place simultaneously to keep up with the ruthless development schedule. For example, the engine design might start on durability testing while the quest for more power—or improved drivability—is still ongoing. If there are big changes, the tests might have to be done again, but it's likely that at least some of the parts will have been proven, thereby simplifying the remaining

LEFT: Suzuki completely revised the GSX-R1000's frame for 2005. Now made up mostly of high-pressure cast components, it is lighter, shorter, and more rigid than before. New casting techniques mean the company can produce more of the frame in cast material, which saves weight and shortens assembly time. Suzuki took every opportunity to improve the product, at the same time making it easier to build.

RIGHT: Suzuki applied new casting techniques to the swingarm as well. For 2005, the forward section is now cast instead of being made out of welded aluminum sheet. In addition, castings replace the long extrusions that made up the bulk of the previous arm.

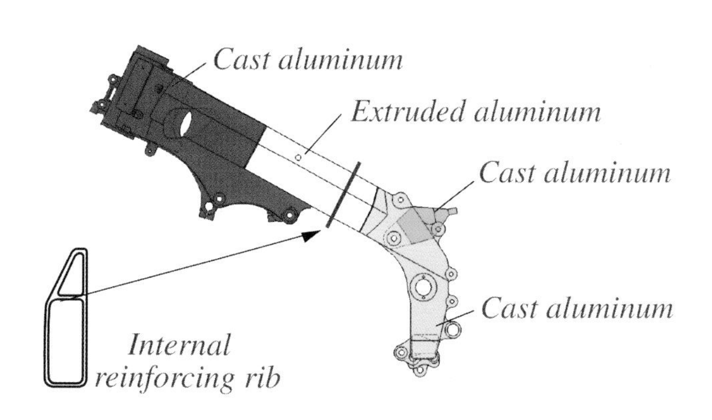

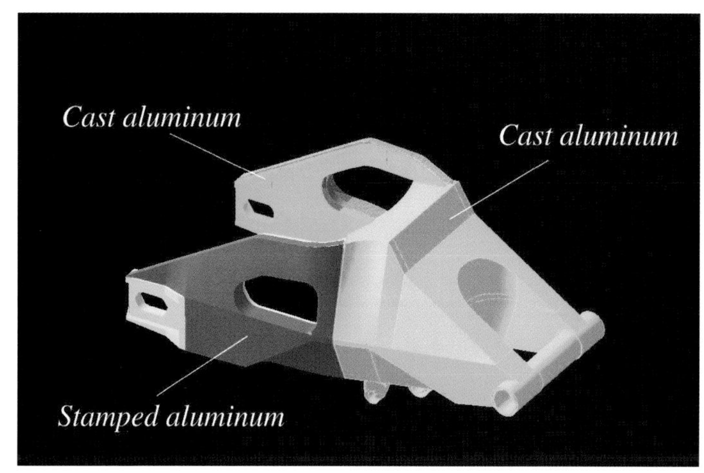

BELOW AND RIGHT: Suzuki's talented—and, from the enthusiast's point of view, extremely lucky—test riders are Atsushi Murata (below) and Yuichi Nakashima (right). They are among the many men whom you can thank for an exceptionally good-handling GSX-R1000.

tests. Like most manufacturers, Suzuki's engineering teams will run the engines and drivelines nearly to destruction, and sometimes beyond, to prove their durability.

As more representative examples come together, such as a chassis that is close to spec and an engine that is nearly the final item, the test riders start their work in earnest. Thankfully, the GSX-R line is well proven, and like any good race team, the development riders have their notes and data from previous bikes to start from. In other words, they don't have to reinvent much when a new model arrives. Through testing and experience, they know the approximate spring and damping rates, for example, and they appreciate that certain changes in chassis geometry or weight distribution will have certain influences on handling.

Atsushi Murata and Yuichi Nakashima are the lucky men whose job it is to pound around Ryuyo, day after day, on fabulously quick and competent motorcycles. Their work is, as you'd expect, methodical. They will test various suspension setups and rate them on a gradated scale. They will try different brake configurations and rate them. They will romp around the track and sample different injection maps and rate them. On and on it goes, working through the matrix of possibilities, coming to conclusions about the bike you will someday own. Any good war tales? They look at each other. "We almost always agree," says Mr. Murata.

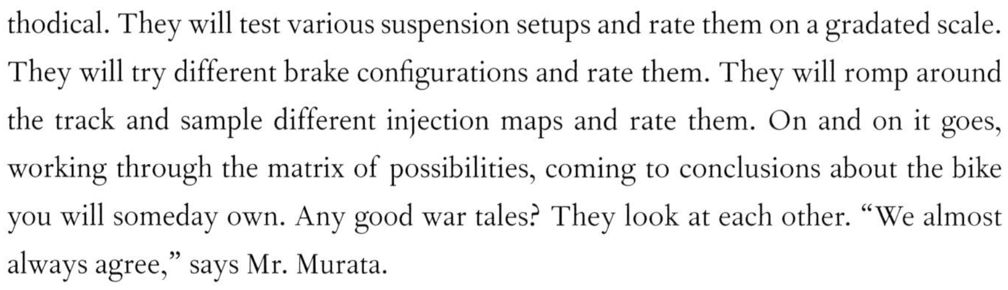

Perhaps most interesting is that, after all the data collection, computer simulations, and dyno time, it comes down to these unpresupposing men to decide what works best. And it's not just them. Much of the development happens behind the gates at Ryuyo, but final settings are determined after riding on other tracks and on the street. For the GSX-R series, the bulk of the development happens in Europe. The bikes are brought to the U.S. before the official launch to double-check that they work well on American roads. At that point, however, much of the development is done, and the changes are minimal. "Normally, the change is only to the recommended suspension settings," says Mr. Murata.

This entire process—development of technology, initial testing, production testing, durability testing, and, finally, test riding to figure out if the product is as good as the numbers say—all has to take place at an accelerated rate. Starting with a good platform helps the process; beginning anew each generation is for other manufacturers with much larger engineering staffs. Indeed, Suzuki's engineers and product planners—safe to say, everyone involved in motorcycle development—are intensely proud that they've done so much with a comparatively small staff. That the 2005 GSX-R1000 is such a leap from its celebrated predecessor is testament to their tireless efforts.

LEFT: Emissions testing takes place on all new models in a facility Suzuki built just for this purpose. This is a station inside the Ryuyo facility used for development and verification before production begins. **BELOW:** In one dyno room at the Ryuyo facility, a GSX-R1000 Superbike engine undergoes a detailed development plan. Every race engine spends time on the dyno in the quest for maximum horsepower, but development continues on the racetrack to find the best compromise between pure power and power delivery.

ABOVE: Suzuki is a vertically integrated company, but not only in the ways that you'd think. The facility has two stories in the main buildings to preserve land space, so elevators are used to move motorcycles to and from the second floor. **RIGHT:** Suzuki has a specially built "cold room" for testing bike performance at very low temperatures. For this test, the bike has to start at temperatures as low as –20°C (–4°F) and idle reliably.

SUZUKI

CHAPTER 9

CAN WE MAKE ONE FOR YOU?

OPPOSITE: On the day your GSX-R1000 was born, the assembly line at Toyokawa was warmed up with a run of GSX-R750s. Suzuki's advanced production capabilities make line changes efficient, which in turn maximizes plant output and overall production flexibility.

BELOW: A large part of Suzuki's production efficiency is the use of just-in-time concepts. These carts carry subassemblies to the line, and can be moved up to the assembly line for the start of a new run, or just as easily pulled away into staging areas when the line changes over to another model.

It should be amply clear that the technology behind every GSX-R—from the original 1985 machine to today's range of three race-ready Superbikes—is not just impressive but carefully planned to allow Suzuki to build the GSX-Rs and sell them into an incredibly price-sensitive market. Beyond Suzuki's traditional traits—making the most of its engineering dollars by, in part, connecting the production and racing cycles at close intervals—is the fact that the company has worked extremely hard to streamline the actual production of the machines.

How quick, and how efficient? Consider this fact: at the end of the assembly line at the Toyokawa plant in the Aichi Prefecture, one sparkling new GSX-R rolls off the end—under its own power—every fifty-six seconds. It takes a mere forty-five minutes from the initial assembly procedure on the main line—fitting the bare frame onto a machine that simultaneously presses in the steering-head bearing cups and stamps the vehicle identification number (VIN)—to the very first running of the engine under the heat of combustion. To consider this feat from the perspective of your easy chair is to be surprised and, perhaps, amused; to be on the floor at Toyokawa and watch it happen is to be astonished.

Such production savvy comes from a long history of assembly-line evolution and a full-bodied embrace of "just-in-time" manufacturing. This process dramatically reduces the amount of product that must be stored at the assembly plant and increases efficiency by an equally dramatic amount. What's more, just-in-time is designed for quick turnover in the production line, so that batches of a given product can be made in the precise size to match any number of variables, including market demand (global or regional), shipping ability, and even seasonality. With this system, a manufacturer is not locked into producing a given number of a particular product on a predetermined schedule. In fact, this is an amazingly fluid environment, where variables can be accommodated without a hitch.

Typical of modern manufacturers, many of the GSX-R's components come from outside vendors—Keihin for the fuel injection, Showa or Kayaba

(KYB) for the suspension, Tokico or Nissin for the brakes, and on down the line. In Japan, the manufacturer/vendor relationship is strongly rooted and carefully nurtured, while at the same time it's well known that competition keeps everyone performing to the maximum.

All of this is beneath the surface when you're confronted with the massive realities of series production. The Toyokawa plant is a densely packed beehive of activity that proceeds at an orderly yet boisterous pace. No one ever seems to be running from one place to another in a flat panic, but you will not see anyone (besides visiting journalists) standing around.

Where, precisely, your motorcycle first begins to take shape—even, actually, when—depends on your point of view. If you view it as centering on the engine, then the first sparks of life begin in the massive engine-assembly plant adjacent to Suzuki's headquarters outside the city of Hamamatsu.

All machining operations are performed at Suzuki, as are component subassembly and final assembly. This is not a one-man, one-engine process. For example, after machining, the cylinder heads follow a separate line that sees the valves and guides installed, followed by the camshafts. Bottom-end work continues on its own line. The engine final assembly takes place in much the same way as the motorcycle assembly (which is described in this chapter) with a final inspection of the engine accompanied by a "running" of the engine by means of an external electric motor. This test ensures that the engine has compression and doesn't make any nasty sounds, but it is done without the engine really running. That will take place later.

Meanwhile, at the main assembly plant, your motorcycle is starting to take life as the components of the frame. (Some of the frames in the accompanying photographs are for the Hayabusa, but the basic process is the same for the GSX-R1000.) Suzuki uses robotics wherever it makes sense and currently employs robotic welding machines in the frame shop. Look at the outside of the main robotic welding apparatus and you'll be hard-pressed to tell what's happening inside. Spools of welding wire as big as 55-gallon drums line the walkway outside the machine, and you can just see the wire being pulled up into the mystery machine at a prodigious rate. Inside the great machine, robotic welders tackle the majority of the frame welds, with the exception of a few segments inside the frame that cannot be reached by the welding head (those will be done by hand afterward). Of course, all of these operations are controlled by computer and carefully designed and monitored so that each frame is properly and accurately welded.

And though it's tempting to believe that machines are better than people, the fact is that the GSX-R frame emerges from the robotic welding system into the hands of skilled workers who visually inspect every weld on the frame and perform any touch-ups required.

The next step is to place the frame back into the hands of a quality-assurance technician to

LEFT: Each and every frame is placed on a series of jigs to check dimensional accuracy.
BELOW: Shock assemblies arrive from the subcontractor ready to be installed.

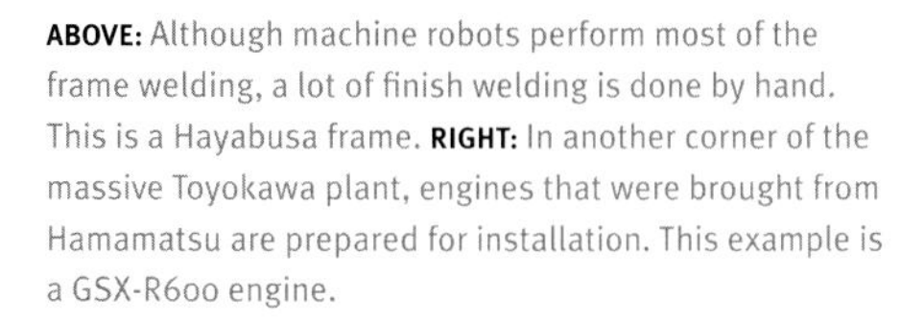

ABOVE: Although machine robots perform most of the frame welding, a lot of finish welding is done by hand. This is a Hayabusa frame. **RIGHT:** In another corner of the massive Toyokawa plant, engines that were brought from Hamamatsu are prepared for installation. This example is a GSX-R600 engine.

修正品

verify that it is dimensionally faithful to the plans. The frame is placed freely on a padded table and checked from point to point using standardized fixtures, which look as though they could be templates derived from NASCAR. One set of these, for example, makes sure that the machined holes on each side of the frame—engine mounts, swingarm pivot, subframe mounts—are aligned. Another fixture checks to see if the distance from the swingarm-pivot holes to the threaded upper-tank mount holes is the correct distance.

OPPOSITE: Again, much handwork is performed on the frames, including hand-polishing of the alloy to finish the welds. This is a Hayabusa frame being finished.

From there, the frame travels a few feet to a station where it is checked for cracks and voids by being sprayed with a red dye penetrant. The exterior coating is removed, and the frame is visually inspected for any remaining dye. The dye will remain in any cracks and be clearly visible when the surface is cleaned.

Perhaps the most surprising part of the frame-welding area is the amount of finish work performed after the frame is actually built. The frame arrives at a series of stations where workers hand-finish the external welds and use a mild abrasive to dress any nicks or other exterior blemishes. The frame is lightly polished even though it's heading across the factory to be painted. Prepped frames join up in racks of twelve and are taken over to the painting area in another corner of the plant.

Two places in the manufacturing process form the greatest bottleneck for the GSX-R, and they are, not surprisingly, paint and fuel tank manufacturing. "We can meet our production goals with one shift in the assembly area, but the tank manufacturing and paint application are run on two shifts," says Yukio Yano, group leader at the Toyokawa plant.

It's difficult to paint well when you're working on one part at a time, but it's vastly more trying when output must be balanced against quality. At Suzuki, as at most modern manufacturing concerns, application of paint is an automated affair, with tanks and frames hung on an overhead rail and drawn through the various painting processes in steps. A cleaning stage ensures no dust and debris are on the surface. In quick succession, the frames are primed and painted and then placed into a drying chamber. (Outsiders don't get to see the painting process in action, but because it all takes place inside a machine, there's not a lot of thrill to viewing it, anyway.) The finished frames emerge, still on the overhead racks, into a small holding area, where they are returned to the rolling carts. These carts, in turn, are brought over to a staging area at the head of the main production lines.

That covers the frame section, but the fuel tank bottleneck comes both from the primary manufacturing stream *and* painting. Suzuki uses a proprietary stamping technology to build the GSX-R tanks, among other models. Traditionally, a steel fuel tank was built in three or more sections, with a simple stamping creating the bottom plate and symmetrical top plates. These plates are seam-welded together, trimmed, and filed smooth. In fact, Suzuki has machines that can do these processes in successive steps without having to remove the tank from the fixture. The GSX-R tank is made from only two stampings. That much we can tell you, because it's patently obvious to anyone familiar with manufacturing; in other words, there's no other logical way to do it. However, Suzuki uses a special process to perform the top stamping that dramatically reduces blemishes and, at the same time, permits complex shapes to be created in the thin-gauge steel. It's an inscrutable process much like the paint process: sheets of flat steel go on the conveyor belt at one end and a stamped half tank chugs out the other side.

In another corner of the plant, your GSX-R's engine has arrived from Hamamatsu on a massive pallet. According to precise timing of the production schedule, it is pulled down from the pallet and subjected to minor prep work that includes installing any exterior hoses and taping over the inlet tubes to prevent anything from falling in. Then the engine is placed into a large cart, which acts as a staging location. The engine actually heads downstairs via a small powered platform, like a dumbwaiter, and moves in dedicated tunnels under each assembly line. When the time comes, each engine rises on a powered platform from the basement to a position next to where it will be installed into the frame. Once again, the engine travels the shortest distance possible between incoming pallet and the actual motorcycle.

Meanwhile—a term used often here because so much happens simultaneously—subassembly areas on the periphery of the plant get to work on a host of parts. For example, technicians working for the fuel-injection supplier unpack throttle bodies, inspect them, and fit them with the throttle cables and a few of the sensors. These parts are assembled and staged in rolling carts. When the cart is full, it is wheeled either to another small staging area at the head of the line or directly to the assembly line itself. Timing is so good here that remarkably few carts are in the staging areas.

Other subassemblies are going together elsewhere in the plant, although a few have been completed by the vendors off-site. For example, the suspension supplier will place both fork legs into the lower triple clamp, which is complete with stem, lower bearing, and steering damper. The wheels come shod with tires, already mounted and balanced. The brake rotors are already on the wheels.

At this point in your GSX-R's gestation, all the parts are in the plant and ready to be assembled. But first the line has to be prepared for the GSX-R1000. On our visit, Suzuki was running a selection of sportbikes on the No. 4 assembly line. In the morning, 20th Anniversary GSX-R750s were rolling off the line, about one a minute. Then, just after the lunch break, the line churned out a couple of hours' worth of Hayabusas. (Let's see, one per minute, excluding changeover time; call it 120 units. *On that day.*)

Just-in-time means more than just having the parts arrive in a reasonable amount of time before

LEFT: The first step in a long but swift process: a machine stamps the VIN (vehicle identification number) into the steering-head casting of a finished frame. (This is a Hayabusa frame.)

BELOW: As the VIN is being stamped, the rear subframe is installed. (This is a GSX-R1000 frame.)

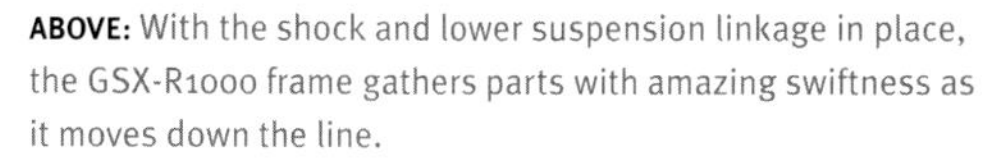

ABOVE: With the shock and lower suspension linkage in place, the GSX-R1000 frame gathers parts with amazing swiftness as it moves down the line.

RIGHT: The engine arrives at the line from an underground passageway. One operator, with the help of an overhead crane, can swing the power plant into place.

the vehicle is to be assembled, but the most amazing part to watch is the line changeover. The main assembly line is just that, a straight line with forty-five stations and people working from both sides. The motorized belt keeps churning except for the twice-daily ten-minute breaks. The moving line is the focus of all the work, with the technician stations flanking it and the supply carts outboard still. It's possible to walk the corridor between assembly lines—Suzuki has six parallel lines at Toyokawa—and hardly see what's being assembled inside for all the equipment, parts, and parts trolleys stacked up.

OPPOSITE: While one technician is checking the engine mounts, another installs the fuel-injection rail.

As the last Hayabusa slides down the line toward life, the supply carts that flank the line are pulled one by one. When the technician at one station installs onto the Hayabusa the last part from the cart, the empty cart is pulled out of the way, often within seconds. Behind it, in a smaller staging area, is the replacement cart holding GSX-R components, which is deftly slid into place. Stand back and you can find where the last Hayabusa is on the line by watching for a flurry of moving carts.

On this day, Suzuki left two spots in the line open between the last 'Busa and the first GSX-R ... all of two minutes.

The painted frames arrive at the main assembly line on large carts that hold approximately a dozen frames. Your GSX-R's frame is pulled from this cart and placed into a fixture that sets the steering-head bearing cups into the frame itself at the same time a computerized punch inscribes the cast steering-stem area with the motorcycle's VIN. This process takes less than thirty seconds. But while the VIN punch is doing its thing, the GSX-R's rear subframe is hoisted over from another cart and bolted into place. The technicians take great care starting the subframe bolts; it's not at all about shoving the fastener into the hole and following it with the pneumatic wrench. Instead, they start the threads by hand while manually supporting the subframe.

Immediately adjacent to the first operation is a technician who expertly places the main wiring harness. Actually, it sounds harder than it is, considering not a lot is attached to the frame just yet. The next step is for one of the technicians to pick up the frame/subframe combination and place it, upside down, into the first segment of the moving line. The frame is held in place through the steering head and rests by the seat mount boss atop a urethane pad.

From this point on, the frame starts taking on parts at an almost dizzying rate. Swingarm assemblies—with the chain, chain guard, and threaded axle adjusters—wait by the line. One worker places the swingarm in place while another slides the axle home. A quick rap with the impact socket and the deal is done. Immediately after, the shock linkage is bolted to the frame and to the swingarm, and before you can turn and say, "Look at that," the shock itself has been plucked out of a massive bin full of them and slid down into the frame with the top clevis already in place. When did that happen?

At about the same time, another technician takes one of the GSX-R1000's titanium mufflers off the cart. It comes with the SET valve installed in the lead-in pipe and cabling already attached. It is bolted loosely to the footpeg bracket to allow for the later installation of the main exhaust system. Also while the frame is upside down, other components are bolted in place, such as the sidestand and the footpeg carriers with the shift linkage and rear-brake master cylinder already in place. Wiring connectors' strategic placement allows the technicians to connect items such as brake-light switches and sidestand-interlock switches without missing a beat.

Soon after these steps are completed, the frame is righted and placed on a second, separate moving line. Now, with the swingarm in position and located by the shock, the bike can be supported by the threaded bosses in the swingarm that will eventually hold your track-stand spools. Supporting the front of the frame is the fork/front wheel assembly, which has been pulled from a cart carrying the preassembly. In this case, the wheel, tire, fender, and brake calipers are already in place, as are the steering damper and lower triple clamp. Just as the frame is reaching horizontal from being flipped right side up, a technician expertly slides the steering stem up through the frame and places the top bearing races, spacer, and threaded collar in place.

The bike continues down the line, gaining clip-on handlebars—which are, as you can guess, already assembled with switches, levers, perches, front-brake master cylinder, and handgrips. The handlebars are left loose for the time being.

A station or two down the line, the frame is ready for the engine. From the staging area, the engine travels underground and appears, on time, at a small platform to the right side of the bike. An overhead crane arrangement allows a single worker to grab the engine by means of horizontal prongs, heft it off the platform, and bring it carefully—but quickly—under the main-frame rails and into position. It takes longer to read about it than to do it.

The engine mounts to the frame with the help of threaded spacers. Those castellated nuts you see surrounding the engine-mount bolts are there to accommodate engine-to-engine and frame-to-frame variances. The engine is slid into place and the mounting bolts are driven in. Then the castle-head adjusters are driven tight. This process makes the engine installation go very quickly. While a pair of technicians places the engine in the frame, others install the chain over the countershaft sprocket and hook up the engine wiring harness to the main harness.

Next in line, the throttle body assembly is placed on the engine and connected electrically. A pair of technicians maneuver the exhaust headers into place and bolt them down with an ease that makes all of us who have fought with pipes feel like dullards. At the next station, a technician uses a pivoting fixture to bring the rear wheel over to the bike. With practiced hands, he slides the wheel in

ABOVE LEFT: A special fixture lifts the rear wheel and helps guide it into position. The technician does not actually lift the weight of the wheel. **BELOW LEFT:** A technician works to install the header pipe. The muffler and SET valve are left loose on the right side to facilitate this maneuver. **FAR LEFT:** With the radiator and oil cooler installed as a unit, the forward fairing can be installed; it arrives at the line already bolted to the instrument cluster and mount.

ABOVE: Now that the engine is in place, the chain can be set over the countershaft sprocket, and the cover installed. **RIGHT:** Before the forward fairing goes on, the steering damper is bolted down.

BELOW: After testing for leaks in a shallow bath, the fuel tank is installed.

place while a worker on the other side drives the axle into place. (Now you know why Suzukis have the axle nut on the left side.) A quick jab with the impact driver and the nut is tight.

Soon after the bike gets a rear wheel and an exhaust system, the radiator and oil cooler—packaged as a set with the cooling fan—arrive on the bike. Now with the coolant and oil systems sealed up, they can be filled, a process that's done automatically through overhead supply lines that are flexible enough to be able to follow the bike as it moves down the line. Speaking of fluids, at this point a worker installs the brake lines and then, some steps down the line, another worker, again with automatic equipment, fills the systems with fluid. The brake fluid is provided under pressure, and there's no bleeding of the brakes from the caliper side.

Another worker installs the airbox assembly, and the bike is ready for the fuel tank. On a side line, painted fuel tanks are lined up on moving carts. A small subassembly line immediately adjacent to the main line installs the combination bottom plate/fuel pump/level sender apparatus. The tank is then dipped into a shallow bath and a small amount of air pressure is applied (less than 1 psi) while the technician looks for bubbles. Seeing none, the tank is hoisted out of the pool, dried briefly, and placed on the motorcycle. Once the fuel lines and electrical connections have been made, the tank is bolted down and the gas cap is installed. The key, which has been in the ignition all this time, is checked to see that it works in the newly installed cap. Then the bike is filled with a small amount of fuel—just enough to pressurize the injection pump and injectors and run the bike at the end of the line.

With the tank in place and most major systems serviced and ready for action, your GSX-R starts getting its bodywork. As expected, the fairings are preassembled in areas surrounding the main assembly lines and so are ready to go when they reach the carts. When bodywork is installed it is quickly covered with a protective pad to prevent scrapes and scratches that might result from the remaining assembly tasks. The forward fairing is installed complete with the instruments, ram-air ducts, and mirrors already in place. One quick click on an electrical connector and a couple of bolts through the fairing bracket, and your motorcycle has a face.

The lower fairings are a bit more involved, because small air deflectors around the radiator must be installed. Still, it's the work of just a few seconds, and soon the side panels are in place as well. Next comes the passenger saddle. The rider's saddle is left off for the moment so that a technician can hook the battery leads to an overhead cable that provides 12 volts to the motorcycle. At this time, the ignition is turned on and the lights checked for the first time.

Work on your bike now slows appreciably, with quality-assurance inspectors starting to take over. Every surface is checked for blemishes, and any small nicks and scratches are buffed out on the spot. (There are remarkably few of these.)

OPPOSITE: The side fairings are installed. On a small side station, the inner fairing panels have been screwed into place just a few seconds before the main panel is needed on the line.

BELOW: A bin full of passenger saddles is among the last large containers on the tour.

A small auxiliary battery is pulled from a cart, and its leads are clipped to the bike's battery cables. Once again, the lights are checked, the horn honked, and the instruments scrutinized for the proper indications. The next step is to roll the bike off the rear stand and onto both wheels for the first time. At this point, the bike is off the rolling assembly line, which has conspicuously fewer stations per foot of track, so that the inspectors at the end of the line have more time to do their critical jobs.

Rolling now but still not alive, the bike is pushed over a pneumatic center stand that hoists the bike off the ground so the wheels can be checked for freedom of movement, and the steering head is checked from lock to lock. This step takes ten or fifteen seconds.

The next phase in the motorcycle gestation is perhaps the most exciting for onlookers but seems utterly routine for the workers. The bike is rolled over to an in-ground dyno. The worker turns on the ignition again, grabs the clutch lever, and ... lights the fire. Your fuel-injected GSX-R wakes immediately into a smooth, even idle. A puff of blue smoke—the result of assembly lubrication burning off in the no-longer-virgin combustion chambers—wafts a foot or so before it is sucked up into a collector that has risen from the floor behind the bike. The technician gives your GSX-R a gentle prod or two of the throttle and pushes a button to lock the front wheel into a special chock so that the rear wheel is centered over the rollers in the floor. Now, with the engine alive for perhaps ten or fifteen seconds, the technician pops it into first gear, lets out the clutch, and sets the rear wheel in motion. There's no look of concern on his face. Is everything tight in there? Did anyone forget a step?

Nothing. Rev it up in first gear, then grab second. Then third. Fourth. Fifth and sixth, and then a short run in top gear at what is later explained is between 80 and 100 kph (50 and 60 mph). Call it 4,500 rpm, max. The technician quickly checks an overhead monitor that shows the results of the test. Then, clutch in, click-click back through to neutral. (He gets it the first time.) Another check of the lights and horn, and he pushes the button that drops the chock.

Once more into first gear, the bike is driven under its own power—all of a hundred feet or so—to the final inspection station. With the engine not yet up to temperature, the muffler still cool to the touch, your GSX-R is shut off for the last time in the land of its origin.

There's no time for reflection. Your GSX-R is moved to a short line where the fuel is removed (and recycled, naturally) and the rider's saddle bolted in place. Another set of quick inspections—including one under bright lights to look for leaks and assembly miscues—and the bike is ready

LEFT: There are fewer stations at the end of the line to space out the arrival of the bikes and allow the quality-assurance inspectors time to do their jobs. **BELOW:** Paint guns stand at the ready in case a bike needs a small amount of touch-up. Seldom is that required.

ABOVE: It's alive! With a seeming nonchalance about the new life being born (he has done this hundreds of times before, just like any seasoned obstetrician), the technician at the end of the main production line starts your bike for the first time. **RIGHT:** The bike is hoisted over to the waiting crate frame.

for crating. In preparation for this, thin sheets of protective material are placed on the bodywork and a support is installed into the hollow swingarm pivot.

The crate is literally built around the motorcycle. A baseplate is pulled onto a rolling line, and the motorcycle is hoisted up and over to the plate, where it is quickly secured. Then the thin metal sides of the crate are built up around the bike as various paperwork is placed alongside the bike. The windscreen is added to the crate, and a cardboard cover is readied and then gently lifted over the bike. It is secured to the metal base by machine screws.

It's a short forklift ride from the end of the crating line to the small warehouse in back, but not many bikes stay home for long. In fact, the GSX-R1000 we watched start out as a collection of parts—perhaps *your* GSX-R1000—was forklifted directly to a waiting truck for shipment to the port.

From the moment the VIN puncher first kissed its steel into the soft aluminum frame until the bike was loaded onto the truck—oil still slightly warm, coolant in the radiator just starting to mix with the warmer antifreeze from the water jackets—astoundingly little time passes.

Seventy-five minutes. Give or take.

BELOW: Still warm to the touch, your packaged GSX-R is forklifted through a small holding warehouse to await a truck—chances are it won't be there long—that will carry it to the shipping port before the bike goes on to its final destination.

STOP

TWENTY YEARS AND STILL PUSHING HARD

The author's lasting impressions from Japan

OPPOSITE: The sun sets in Ryuyo only to rise again on another day of strenuous motorcycle development. The overarching impression from a visit to the proving grounds is that the engineers never rest, never allow an innovation to pass them by—which means great new ideas will appear in each succeeding generation of GSX-R being developed.

BELOW: It says a lot about Suzuki as a company that many of the engineers involved in the original GSX-R remain dedicated to the model. The author (blue shirt) confers with the engine-development team during extensive interviews with the men behind the GSX-R.

In modern business, the term *corporate culture* is used rather too casually. It's defined as "the collection of beliefs, expectations, and values shared by an organization's members and transmitted from one generation of employees to another." What this definition fails to specifically include is *drive*. Motivation. Why is this bright young designer working twelve-hour days to get a fairing detail just right? Why is this veteran engineer also putting in twelve-hour days to shave a gram of weight from a part or extract an extra tenth of a horsepower from an engine?

If you'd never met either of these men you might be quick to assume the motivation is to keep a job, to do well enough to move up the ladder and retire with a nice fishing boat. But I have met these men and can tell you that there's something more, particularly for those intimately involved with the GSX-R. (And it's true that the motocross engineers, and ATV designers are just as driven in their quest to develop their products.) The product is crucial, of course, and winning races, earning the praise of the press, and selling lots of units are all among the motivations you'd expect. Still, there was something more, and it took a few days to figure it out—days of talking to the engineers and designers, seeing motorcycles being built, watching the test riders run hard around the test track at Ryuyo on semi-damp pavement with the confidence born of thousands of laps on all kinds of motorcycles.

Finally it occurred to me: harmony. Because of the unique nature of the GSX-R concept—with its crystal-clear intent and plainly stated goals—it is, today, easy for everyone to pull in the same direction. A successful GSX-R is one that is faster and better handling, in general a better *performer*, than its competition. It does not strive to be the one bike for every rider. It does not need outlandish styling. It need not embody trendy technology.

This GSX-R, boiled to essence, is an intensely straightforward machine. All it has to do is perform. It's the performance that sells. And wins races.

Talk to the engineers, many of whom are still with the company after twenty years and who are delighted to discuss development of the original GSX-R in the way of proud parents, and you get a sense of the intensity. Computers allow the engineers to work just as breathtakingly hard but be more productive. Still, they push on.

These engineers inhabit offices at the Ryuyo complex, in which Suzuki motorcycles share space with the automotive and marine divisions—although the facility is primarily for motorcycles as the car and marine sectors use the facility only for testing purposes. The MotoGP team is housed there, too, working in the lab and on the dynos well into the night. One part of our tour allowed us into a dyno facility. In one cell, where a Superbike engine was undergoing development, several of the tiny cylinder heads from the GSV-R MotoGP bike were stacked in a corner. If you were ever to think that engine development was simply a matter of designing on the computer, sending the file to the CNC machine to create the ideal part, and thence to the track, you would be very much wrong. Every improvement in the engine comes on the back of hours of testing—methodical and precise and never-ending. Near the end of the tour, one of the dyno technicians could be seen idly playing with an exhaust pipe for the GSV-R engine. His expression was enigmatic, but you just knew he was waiting with as much patience as he could muster for us to leave so he could get back to work and find that extra half a horsepower.

Scenes like this played out all over Suzuki: in Ryuyo, at the manufacturing plant in Toyokawa, and at the headquarters in Hamamatsu. The overarching impression is one of a singularity of focus. The development pace is harsh, but the men behind the GSX-R are clearly up to it. Clarity plays a big role in the motivation. There is no part of the GSX-R's strength and success that is not utterly understood by all.

And the future of the GSX-R? No intelligent vehicle manufacturer gives away its product plans, but enthusiasts can expect the brand to continue on its current rapid development cycle—a move that keeps all of us looking forward to ever-better motorcycles and, much to Suzuki's pride, ensures that its competition cannot ever relax. Racing, likewise, will continue to inform the designs. Lessons learned on the track will be put back into the street bikes, in turn, making them better track bikes and platforms for production-based racing. With the recent consolidation of the R & D department at Ryuyo, expect to see the race/production gap narrow and innovations from both Superbike and MotoGP efforts arrive in a showroom near you.

One thing all enthusiasts should expect is that the GSX-R will remain faithful to its mission. After two decades of development, the GSX-R isn't just well understood in the Suzuki culture, it *is* the Suzuki culture.

BELOW: While the GSX-R1000 was conceived as a racing platform and developed on racetracks around the world (as well as at Suzuki's own test track), the performance-minded street rider was never far from the engineers' thoughts. A modern sportbike must be fast, of course, but confidence inspiring as well—it's this last characteristic that's most difficult to develop, but well worth the effort.

ACKNOWLEDGMENTS

ABOVE: It's easy to focus on the exciting hardware when considering the 2005 GSX-R1000 and the trend-setting series of motorcycles that preceded it. But the GSX-R is more than the sum of its technological parts because of the people and personalities that created it. If we learned anything from our time in Hamamatsu it's that the passion for performance is as influential as thoughtful engineering.

There are so many people who generously gave their valuable time to contribute to the research for this book that it's hard to know where to start. Perhaps at the beginning—in Japan. I would like to thank every member of the Suzuki Motor Corporation team for sitting through endless questions and offering intimate and exciting perspectives on all things GSX-R. During our time in Japan, publisher David Bull and I were warmly greeted and provided the kind of insider access that is seldom seen in modern manufacturing. On our first evening, Suzuki executives Masayoshi Ito, Masami Haga and Takeshi Hayasaki took us to the first of what would be many dinners memorable for both the lively conversation and tremendous cuisine. I would also like to thank Sadayuki Inobe and Hironori Iguchi, Suzuki veterans both, for their contributions to this work. My heartfelt thanks to Suzuki's engineering and styling-design staff at Ryuyo and the Hamamatsu headquarters for their insights and wonderful recollections of the first, the intermediate, and the latest GSX-Rs.

I would also like to specifically thank Etsuo Yokouchi for his time and energy, without which this book would not embody the complete GSX-R story. I would be remiss if I didn't thank Kazuhiro Shiratori and Ryo Shimono, both members of the motorcycle planning department in Japan, who were invaluable to us in negotiating our way through the Suzuki home office and archives, the Ryuyo testing facilities, the Toyokawa assembly plant, and Hamamatsu traffic, as well. Their organization, stamina, and enthusiasm were exemplary and critical to the success of the book.

Back at home, I'd like to thank Glenn Hansen and Garrett Kai of American Suzuki Motor Corporation for their tremendous behind-the-scenes support, including coordinating interviews, photos and artwork, and vetting facts. They were the human equivalent of traction control for what is inevitably a large and sometimes careening project.

Huge props to Tom Morgan and Laura McBride of Blue Design, who pulled off another triumph of style married to substance in the design of this book. Once again we were on what can only be described as brutally tight deadlines and, once again, Tom and company came through with a beautiful piece of work.

And I'd like once more to thank my wife Martha and daughter Millie for their understanding and, in particular, the constant stream of support (and lattes) arriving at my desk at all hours.

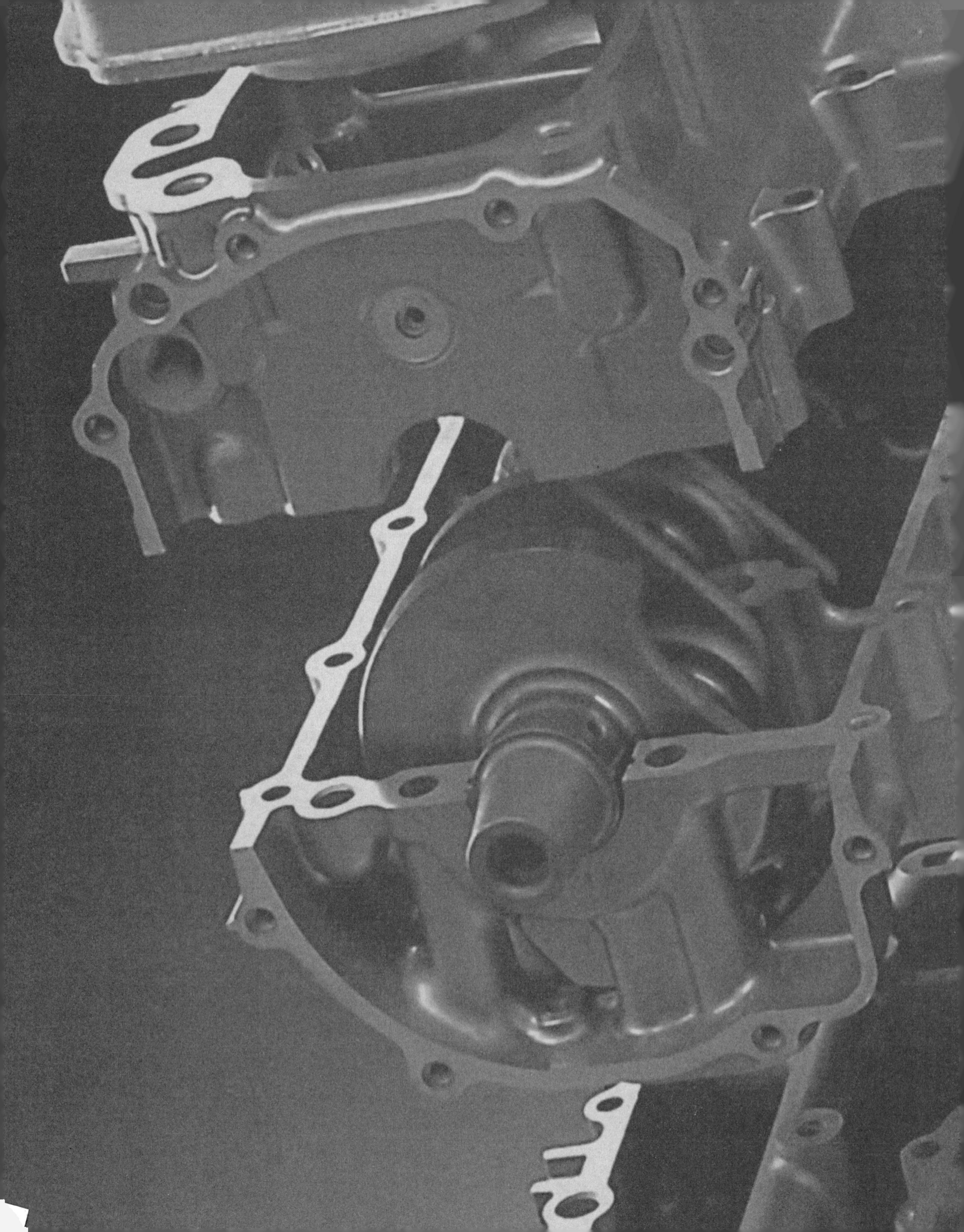